CW00672380

A Hebridean Journey

The Travel Diary

of

Isabell Burton MacKenzie

First published in Great Britain in 2020

Thanks are due in no small measure to Dr John MacInnes for supplying the foreword to this book

ISBN 978-0-9957205-6-5

Publishing,
Typesetting & design by
Hamilton House Publishing Ltd.

Rochester Upon Medway,
Kent.

Isabell Alicia Eva Burton MacKenzie
1872-1958

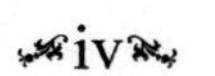

Introduction

Isabell Alicia Eva Burton MacKenzie was born in Union Street Aberdeen on 6 October 1872. She died on 9 May 1958 in Gartnavel Hospital, Glasgow. She begins her Diary of her Hebridean journey in August 1912 , giving the address as, Kilcoy Castle on the Black Isle, her family home.

Spinster ladies leave few traces in history and because her diary has survived her, we have this unique snapshot into her remarkable journey in the Western Isles, the Scottish Highlands and the Mainland of Scotland.

The Highland Home Industries Board was formed in 1907, and with it's headquarters in Edinburgh this remained a showcase for craft work from the whole of Scotland until it's demise in the late twentieth century. The knitting in the Highlands and Western Isles and the formation of The Highland Home Industries Limited developed alongside the Harris Tweed Industry. The overall aim of this body was to raise the standard of Home Industry particularly in the remote Outer Isles, focussing in 1912 on North and South Uist, Eriskay, Barra and Skye.

Miss Isabell Burton-McKenzie was appointed as their Travelling Organiser from 1911-14. She was a woman of vision and although untrained in business methods, her diary shows an empathetic attitude to the workers and people. She had learnt the Gaelic Language as an essential means of communicating directly with the people. Very little English was spoken at that time by the crofters and fisherfolk and usually confined to dealings with the merchants, the Church and landlords. The paradox or anomaly here is that by the 1930s Gaelic was forbidden in schools and children were physically punished if they spoke their native language, whereas at the turn of the century the peasant was regarded as a noble savage and the upper classes regarded helping them as some kind of redemption for the ruthless actions of their land owning ancestors.

The people of the Outer Hebrides from North Uist to Barra carried living memories of scenes of the most brutal episodes of the Clearances from the evictions in the 1850s. to the more recent land Raids of Barra and Vatersay, in the first decade of the twentieth century. These were economically fragile communities whose livelihoods depended on the land and sea. The weather in these islands, especially in the Autumn and Spring Equinoxes is extreme, especially when the full force of Atlantic Gales is experienced. The diary and account book covers the months from August to December 1912 and she notes only two fine calm days in this period.

From her diligent account, Isabell appears as an intrepid, eccentric traveller, hiring a pony to visit remote crofts and showing courage when faced with dangerous weather in her journeys by sea and land. A single woman with a sense of humour, able to converse in Gaelic and note the qualities of the people and children she met with shrewd wit and kindness. She enjoyed a game of golf, walking and conversing.

Isabell illustrates her account with remarkable pen and ink sketches and photographs giving a unique glimpse into a vanishing world.

Foreword

We have numerous collections of poetry, music and folktales made over the last two or three centuries in the Highlands and Islands of Scotland. By way of contrast, however, we have few descriptions of the everyday life of the people who contributed to these collections. As a consequence, every scrap of information is of great interest.

Alyne Jones is to be congratulated for bringing this diary to light. Furthermore, the fieldwork she is planning to carry out should revive memories of a variety of home-based industries which will provide material of enormous value to social historians.

Dr. John MacInnes, 20 April 2016.

The Original diary resides in the Vanishing Scotland Archive and is available as a Facsimile Edition. The first page shown here, illustrates the quality of her photographs and her insightful comments.

The layout and typography of the book may appear eccentric but it faithfully represents the pagination and layout of the original diary, which is handwritten in an account book with red lines. These lines appear throughout the book and captions are also as they appear in the original diary. Annotations interspersed throughout the text are indicated by a different font.

1.

On "SS. Hebrides crossing the Minch

Exiles from Uist

The little girl of about 13 - "Morag" - has won a Bursary & is going to School in Glasgow - to live in lodgings among utter strangers -

This is the first time she has been on a Steamer - she has never seen a Train - never seen a Tree - never seen a Town - and had never seen her fellow-travellers before.

This is a happier family party returning home to the father in Glasgow after their holiday on the grandparents' croft in the Outer Isles.

Contents

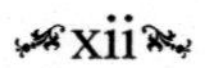

A Hebridean Journey

The Diary of Isabell Burton MacKenzie

Kilcoy, Ross-Shire, August 1912.

A flock of best "Black . Faced"
Just come over the South Ford from Benbecula
with a long road before them to Grogorry, South Uist.

Widow MacPherson & little grandchild Morag.

One of the best spinners in South Uist – her arms are full of wool which she going to dye – a year ago she fell & broke her leg so she has to use crutches but it has not spoilt her spinning – .

Clachan. Locheport. Lochmaddy. North Uist.

Thursday 1st. August to Sunday 11th August. 1912.

Aug.1st. 2nd.
I arrived at Kilcoy from London in the afternoon – packed – & started next morning for the Outer Isles – reached Skye (Portree) that night & was obliged to sleep there in order to catch the 6.a.m. Steamer for Lochmaddy, North Uist, which got there on Sat. afternoon –.

3rd
Mr. McElfrish, Sheriff-Clerk, Kindly met me & he had arranged with Fergusson (Merchant in both Lochmaddy & Locheport & Agent for Mrs Stewart MacKenzies' Industries) to get his wife to give me lodgings at Clachan, Locheport – 8 miles West of Lochmaddy – as the house is right in the centre of the spinning and weaving crofting districts.

I drove out there in the evening, first looking at a large quantity of tweed in Mrs Stewart-MacKenzies' Depot at Lochmaddy – it is under the charge of Fergusson's sister – she and he both lamented the slackness of trade & said there has been no demand at all for tweeds this year –

The Tweed Industry and its decline was one of the reasons for the Founding of the Scottish Home Industries under the patronage of H.R.H. The Princess Louise, The Countess of Rosebery being President. Their second exhibition was held in London on Monday 4th July 1898.

In 1897, 65,000 yards of tweed were sold through the Association. Importantly it guaranteed that the Tweed was 'cottage' made and vegetable dyed. The greatest demand was from sporting clients. Riding, shooting and cycling particularly were enjoyed by those in society who had disposable incomes. The main difference the Association made to the Crofters, was that they were paid money directly, instead of the "middlemen" (merchants) taking their cut. The Gaelic speaking crofters were skilled and were able to produce the goods which were sent as far afield as Africa, America & the Far East.

5th.

On Monday I called at half a dozen crofts – two of them with looms – but was a good deal handicapped by having no "cards" or anything to explain my presence – although I made friends with the people and am to go back & see them again – as 2 or 3 were out – in one house the old mother was spinning and her daughter weaving - the latter had only learnt to do it about a year ago & can now make about 8 yards a day – quick weavers can do from 9 to 10 she said.

6th.

Next day Tuesday, I determined to make friends with the authorities in the district – i.e. Rev. Euan Gillies, U.F. Manse (the Established Minister being miles away), Fergusson himself, my landlord, and Maclean, Merchant, Carinish, all of whom tell the same story, no sale this year for the tweeds. –

The Minister and Fergusson both think that the recent Lawsuits have done the damage, especially the "Trade Mark" one, but Maclean declares it is the Lewis people who have flooded the market with "Machine – spun – Homespuns" and are underselling the people of Uist and Harris – He told me that in Lewis they can make a good profit by selling as low as 2/6 per yard – while 2/10 is the lowest price a profit can be made out of here – the reason being that a web of 60 yards which will take the best Uist spinner over 2 months to turn out, can be put on the market in one week by the Lewis worker – the Lewis workers get the mill-spun wool over from the Mills in herring-barrels & then quickly weave it – .

I asked him if he could tell the difference, he answered he knows but would not like to swear – – I gathered from him that a very little of the mill spun wool has begun to creep into Uist too – he is a merchant who has practically made his fortune out of the Homespuns and is very proud of having started the Industry – or rather the idea of selling the tweeds out of the Island, 30 years ago – and long before the Scottish Home Industries were ever heard of in Uist – he is, of course, very much against all the Associations & says scornfully, they were going to save the people from the 'greed' of the Merchants! & now infers that they have "killed" the industry between them – .

The Minister, whose brother-in-law he is, says he is one of the straightest men he knows and that he has always dealt fairly with the people – he certainly seems genuinely distressed at the present state of things & talked at great length – so much so that he became difficult to follow & I felt if I took out a notebook he would grow annoyed & stop – the gist of his conversation was that now is the time for all the Associations to combine and work under one management entirely – that it should buy out the merchants i.e. buy any tweeds they still have in stock and prevail upon them to deal no more with the people, & upon the people to deal no more with them – and that it should then proceed to fight the Lewis people and other makers of sham homespuns or Harris-tweeds – by means of the extension of the Trade-mark – so that no real homespun should ever be sold without being stamped with the trade mark – .

At present I think the trade-mark applies only to Harris-tweed (i.e. made in Harris or the other Islands) & not at all to tweed made in the Mainland?

MacLean and others cannot understand why the big tailors in towns should be allowed to charge 6 – 8 – 9 or even 10/- a yard for tweed which the original worker has received only 2/10 or 3/- for – they won't see that each additional buyer or seller must stick on a profit if he is to deal in the stuff at all –

A crofter who gave me a lift in his cart next day talked volubly of the iniquity of the rich local merchants & the miserable pay of the workers – but he was chiefly jealous that a rich man like Fergusson should have Mrs Stewart-Mackenzie's agency instead of some crofters who need the money so much more – and he talked as if the agents made a good deal out of the wool they sell to the people – really – I gather – they give out the wool to the worker & the price of it has to be deducted when the web is brought back ready for sale, and this is controlled by the different associations – .

Fergusson has, in his Store here, (Locheport) quantities of tweeds already paid for by Mrs Stewart-MacKenzie, but, as there is very little selling just now she is buying very little – & meantime work for her is rather at a standstill.

Both associations – as well as the local merchants – complain that workers get wool from one & wool from another & then perhaps sell the finished web to the 3rd – and end by being rather hopelessly entangled–

> Isabell is then in the Islands at a crucial turning point, with instructions to improve the life of the Crofting Communities by encouraging diversification from the making of Tweed such as knitting and other crafts. The Co-operative Council of the Highland Home Industries Association, formed in 1907, have employed her as their first Worker in the Highlands and Islands, but she is very much dependent on her own inner resources.

Starting work this week has consisted a good deal in finding my way – no "cards" – & it being Communion Week (yearly here) have both added to my difficulties – Thursday being Fast Day & Friday & Saturday also days of Church-going. I could not visit any of the workers.

August 10th.

But yesterday Saturday I went into Lochmaddy & saw MacTavish at The Scottish Home Industries Depot & heard some of his views – he says the same – little or no demand for tweeds this year – but he has orders to continue the distribution of wool to be spun, hoping that trade will shortly improve – in his opinion, Irish Homespuns made in Yorkshire! are at the bottom of the mischief – he complained too of the wool difficulty & said often that wool taken from the association is given when ready into the merchants hands as payment of an old debt – The association gives a certain amount of payment in kind, i.e. tea, sugar, and flour, but prefers to pay cash & he showed me his books showing how certainly half the payments are made in money.

This system, called the 'Truck' in Shetland was common throughout the Highlands and Islands. The main shop for comestibles and domestic requirements was often owned by the same Merchant who traded in the hand made goods, and so the necessities of life were often given as payment or part payment. Sometimes this meant that the Crofter did not have the independence of his or her own money, but were in a state of constant debt to the Merchant.

After that I went to see Mr McElfrish (Sheriff-Clerk) & from him got a very good idea of all the districts in Benbecula, South Uist and Barra which I shall have to visit & the names of the people who will help me in the various places –

Owing to the difficulty of finding people at home & to their not knowing me yet, I have arranged to have two meetings this week – one on Tuesday night in the U.F. Church here with the Rev. Gillies & Fergusson to explain things & one in Carinish school on Weds night with MacLean the merchant in the chair – the postman is making the meetings known as he goes his rounds.

I am staying on where I am till Saturday the 17th. & by that time hope to have been to see all the workers in this district and to have them down in the register. So far I have heard of no knitters & no homespun yarn seems to be made.

Rev Gillies, Ferguson, & MacLean, the 2 merchants all consider a Carding-mill is badly needed in North Uist, as the wool is now all sent to Tarbert (Harris) where there is much congestion & so very long delays before it comes back ready for spinning.

South Uist and Barra are mainly Catholic Communities, whilst North Uist, Harris and Lewis are mostly Presbyterian – United Free Church and Church of Scotland.

Travelling, Stationery & Postage Expenses from 1st. August 1912.

Date	Item		s.	d.
August **1st**	Card-Index	6/-		
	Diary	1/6		
	Note-book	1/6	10	0
	Refill for do	6^{d}.		
	postage of parcel	6^{d}.		
2nd	Railway ticket 3rd class, Redcastle to Kyle of Lochalsh		6	1.
"	Steamer Kyle of Lochalsh to Portree		5	0.
3rd	do Portree to Lochmaddy		7	0.
	Porters (whole journey)		2	3
4th	Packet of envelopes	1^{d}.		
	stick sealing-wax	1^{d}.		5
	exercise book	3^{d}.		
	Letters written from 1st Aug. to 11th Aug. —			
	(2) Mrs. MacKenzie, Farmer	2^{d}.		
	E. Tann, Stationer,	1^{d}.		
	Army & Navy, Postcard	½		
	Mrs. Burnley-Campbell	2^{d}.		
	Miss Campbell, Inverinch	1^{d}.		
	Sir Kenneth MacKenzie	1^{d}.		
	Mrs. Stuart-MacKenzie	1^{d}.	1	4½
	(2) S&p. *An Comunn Gàidhealach*	2^{d}.		
	Miss T. MacIntyre	1^{d}.		
	Lady Fowler	1^{d}.		
	Mrs. MacAlister	1^{d}.		
	West Ford Inn	1^{d}.		
	Lady Marjory MacKenzie	1^{d}.		
	Army & Navy	1^{d}.		
	Hiring from Lochmaddy to Clachan must come under next week's expenses as I have not yet been able to get the bill.			
		£ 1-	12-	1½

Sunday 11th. to Sunday 18th. August 1912.
(moved on Saturday 17th from Clachan North Uist
to Westford Inn, Cladach Kirkibost North Uist.)

Sunday 11th. August.
Went to the United Free Gaelic Service and Sacrament on the hillside, 1200 people were expected, but, owing to a bad storm just as the distant ones should have been starting, not half the number came. It was held in a beautiful spot above a small loch & one looked across miles of moorland stretching away to the 2 highest peaks Ben Ea-Val & Ben Lee (?)
Ministers from Stornoway, Tarbert and Benbecula were helping Mr. Gillies.
In the evening wrote my diary for the week and posted it to the Sec early next morning.

Monday 12th. August.
Out all day rode down to Locheport Pier and then onto the furthest end of the town ship 7 miles from Clachan, called at a dozen crofts, each house having at least one spinner and sometimes a weaver as well.
Several from this district have been sending the wool to be carded in Portree owing to the Tarbert Mill taking such a long time doing it, & most of them say that the Portree people do it better.
All the Crofters there, or their fathers or Grandfathers were evicted from Sollus, in the North of this Island, in 1850; they seem a contented community but would like to get better prices for their tweeds.

North Uist was hit hard during the Highland Clearances, and there was large scale emigration from the island to Cape Breton, Nova Scotia, Canada. The pre-clearance population of North Uist had been almost 5,000, though by 1841 it had fallen to 3,870, and has further dwindled to about 1,300 people today.

As it was impossible to visit more houses then I said I would come and meet some more of them in the schoolhouse on Friday evening.
One young weaver – married with three children, had learnt only a year ago from Manderson the Instructor provided by the Crofters' Agency – he took only 4 days to learn and bought his loom from the Agency for £7-15-0., he has now paid off £6.10 by his weaving and hopes to learn to weave Clan tartans (work most of them seem afraid of trying – they say it's so difficult). He had a blanket in the loom when I saw it & had picked up the pattern in the border for himself by looking carefully at another blanket he had – his wife spins, but can't do much as the children are all tiny – although he is only 35 he has scarcely any English –
Is it possible to get any orders for him so that he may pay off the cost of the loom & begin

making a profit? Weaving a plain colour is 4d. per yard & 1d. a yard extra for each additional colour – I thought his web very smooth and even – his address is: – "Simon MacQuarrie. Locheport. North Uist".

In this district most of the husbands and children were dressed in the tweeds spun by the women – they use their own sheeps wool in this way & make much thicker coarser stuff on purpose as it wears longer – they never have enough of their own wool at one time to make a whole long web.

Another interesting household was that of a Mrs Rachel MacPhail a spinner and weaver – the husband and 8 children all weaving her tweed. The 3 youngest are "triplets" of 4 years old – bright sturdy little things , the loom was made by her grandfather for her grandmother & is of course one of the old fashioned kind – she would like more work now the triplets are growing older & the elder girl of 11 will soon be able to help with the spinning.

Tuesday 13th. August.

Went to Cladach Baleshare & did several visits – in a house near the Ford saw Mrs Angus MacDonald and her two daughters all very good spinners – Angus is a prosperous crofter who owns sheep and has built a stone house with a tin roof – they spin their own wool. I saw some very finely spun blue wool just ready to go to the weaver & they have promised to send the web to the St. Andrew's Sale – the only son Roderick makes Horse- Collars & door mats of plaited Bent – excellent collars covered with sheepskin price 5/- – he is to send one to the sale too. – he told me there is one other man in the Island of Baleshare who can make them – the covered collars wear for 12 years and the others for 8. – His address is: – Roderick MacDonald, Carnach, Cladach Baleshare. N. Uist.

Later on in the evening such a storm of wind and rain came that not a soul turned up for my meeting in the Church.

The wind seems to be the greatest enemy they have in North Uist, it sweeps across the Island with nothing to stop it – not a single tree – and few hollows even – just long stretches of heather and peat and numbers of lochs – the houses are all built with very thick walls sloping inwards as they rise in height (like buttresses), the thatch with rounded corners so as not to catch the wind – and further – it is covered with a rough network of rope weighted at the ends with heavy stones – all to keep the roof down.

There are no dykes or fences, so ponies, cows and sheep are usually tethered by a long rope – the latter in pairs like Siamese twins – very uncomfortable for them especially when they get twisted round and one faces East and one West and each wants to eat and walk in her own direction – Some crofters own a couple of sheep only and some a good many but hardly own enough to make them independent of buying wool from the Associations or Merchants – they all declare their own is far better than what they buy – softer and finer.

Widow Fraser, Clachan.

Wednesday 14th. August.
Called on people round about Clachan in the morning – it rained later but cleared up in the evening & my landlord Fergusson kindly drove me to the meeting of workers in Carinish school, – the Rev. Gillies coming with us.

The meeting was supposed to begin at 6. We started from Clachan half an hour late and when we arrived found no one – however after a hitch our Chairman, MacLean, Merchant, Carinish turned up, and we went into the school – the holidays have begun so there was no schoolmaster there – then women began coming one by one at intervals, also one man whose wife spins and son weaves, so he came to represent them, – 18 people counting us all! –

MacLean explained about the Council to them in Gaelic – and then followed an animated discussion on prices of wool, profit to the workers, prospects of sale etc – nearly every one taking part in it and a good deal of wit flying about at the expense of the 2 merchants – who took it very well.

I suggested that while the sale of tweeds is so difficult, just now some of them should turn their attention towards spinning yarn for knitting – they all shook their heads at first and said it would not pay, especially when told it would bring in from 2/6d per lb only – 1lb of yarn they said takes as much wool as a yard of tweed which they may sell for 2/10. – I reminded them that 4d at the very least has to come off this to pay the Weaver – so they would be getting the same price really – & if the yarn was very fine and well spun they might get as much as 2/10 to 3/- per lb. – I showed them a skein of yarn I bought in Gairloch Ross-Shire the other day – and told them they must make it as well as that – each woman present (& the man too) took a sample away with her as a pattern & all promised to try making some – and that they would send it to the St. Andrews Sale as a start – we recommended them to use their own wool and card it themselves, this is easy to do when only a small quantity at a time is wanted and is a further saving of 2d a lb for the carding at the mills – besides freight to & from Harris – MacLean told them that if any of them who had his wool would like to send the finished web to St Andrews, and perhaps win a prize, or , if sold, get a better price than he could give, he would allow them to do so – and would trust them to repay him for the wool when they had the money.

At the end of the evening all gave their names and addresses.

Thursday 15th August.

Drizzling rain most of the day went to the Island of Illary Baleshare, had a lift in a peat cart across the ford. Only managed a few visits as the crofts are separated by so much bog-land and it was difficult to go from one to the other, besides having to be back in time to walk across the Ford before the tide came in. A good many of the people were away in Clachan for the sheep-dipping.

Friday 16th August.

Rain at intervals, visited people in Cladach Baleshare. One household a very sad one, belonging to an old crofter called Robertson, a widower with 3 daughters all deaf and dumb, the eldest being also a helpless invalid, the two younger ones spin very well, but it was a miserably dirty house. In the other end of it lives the old man's nephew with his wife and 5 children, the nephew helping him to work the croft.

In the evening Mr. Gillies drove me down to Locheport School for the meeting there, only half a dozen people including one man (Hector MacDonald an elder in the UF church) appeared at it and he told us the reason was the people hearing I was lodging with Fergusson the Merchant made up their minds I was trying to help him to buy their tweeds cheaper! (the cards would have explained everything & it shows how much they are wanted). Mr. Gillies explained all about the Council, & it was all right and then we went over much the same ground as in Carinish.

Saturday 16th August.

Very heavy rain till about 4. o'clock. Packed for the move to Westford Inn, expected to start at 4 but the cart never came till 6. Time being of little account in the Outer Isles.

In the card index I now have the names and addresses of
41 spinners
10 weavers women who also spin
2 weavers men
3 weavers women who have given up and spin only
1 man who makes horse collars & door mats.

Widow Fraser, Clachan,gave me the following figures as to the cost of producing & the profit made on a web of tweed she had lately sold to the Crofters Agency – (a web that counts as 37 British yards is woven by the weaver as 32 Highland yards – or so she tells me)

	£	s	d
Paid for 1 stone Blackface wool	1	0	0
Paid for 1 stone Cheviot wool	1	4	0
Paid for carding at the Mill		7	0
Paid for Weaving		10	8
Paid for Washing soda & soap		2	0
£	3	3	8.

	£	s	d
The web of 37 yards was sold for	5	4	10
But the cost of making it came to	3	3	8
Profit £	2	1	2.

Sold at 2/10 per yard, cost her 1/8½ per yd.
& she made a profit of 1/1½ per yard.

The work took her about 3 months, this included the time spent in waiting for it to be carded –
At "the wauking" she had to feed the nine women who came to help her & this added to her bill at the merchants but she couldn't say how much!

> Waulking (in Gaelic luadh) is the technique used to finish the newly woven tweed by soaking it and thumping it rhythmically to shrink and soften it.The cloth was soaked in stale urine. This was known in Gaelic as maistir, helping to make the dyes fast, and to soften the cloth. In Uist and Barra, after being waulked the cloth was rolled up, and patted to smooth it out to the accompaniment of a clapping song (oran basaidh) which was a fast, cheerful song, sometimes an improvised "pairing off" song, when the names of those present would be linked with local young men.

Some other women have told me that their net profit on a web of 40 yards – 3 months work – does not amount to more than £1.0.0 , but then another said that she got a Boll of meal from the merchant before she began the spinning and this roughly is valued at £1.0.0. – so that would make the profit again just about £2.0.0. – I have heard vaguely of such and such a woman who is a first rate spinner making 200 yards of tweed in a year - - - thus earning £10. or £2. (at least) less than the old-age-pension. (Widow Fraser has the old age pension and must be rather a rich woman!)

Rachel Morrison. Locheport. showed me a receipt for money paid to the North Harris Carding Mill.

" to carding 20½ lbs wool 3/5 "
" freight to Lochmaddy 6d "

She had to walk a good 10 miles to fetch it from Lochmaddy, carrying it home on her back, or else pay an extra 1/- freight to Locheport Pier.
She said she pays for

"Spanish wool 22/- per stone
"Wool of this country" 18/- do do.

that she mixes them together – and that it requires 8 stone of wool to make 40 Highland yards. (probably about 48 or 49 British yards but I do not yet know the proportions)
Several others have mentioned paying 20/- per stone for wool.

Travelling Stationery & Postage Expenses from 11th August 1912.

	£	s	d
Carried forward from 1st to 11th August.	1	12	1-
Half-share of luggage-cart 3rd Aug. from Lochmaddy to Clachan, 8miles 5/-		2	6
Half-share of luggage-cart 17th Aug. from Clachan to Westford Inn. 3½ miles 2/6		1	3
Hire of Crofter's pony to ride while at Clachan		6	
Stationery :– Staple press 4/6; 500 staples 1/-; Box of paper fasteners 1/-; Blotting-Pad 1/6; Box sealing-wax 2/3; Packet Long envelopes 1/-; Rubber Stamp Co-op. Council 4/-; Postage of Parcel 8d		15	11
"Letter-File"		1	11
packet of small envelopes			1
Posting St Andrew's Sale Rules to John Maclean, Carinish,			1
Reply paid wire to Hon. Sec.		1	
Letters written from 11th Aug. to 18th Aug.: (2) Mr McElfrish 2d; E.Tann, Stationer 1d; Miss Maclean, Benbecula 1d; (3) Hon. Sec. 3d			7
£	3	1	- 5 -

Sunday 18th to Sunday 25th August 1912.
Westford Inn, Cladach Kirkibost, N. Uist.

Sunday 18th

Wrote diary and a number of letters and then discovered no mail would leave till Tuesday morning.

Monday 19th

Stormy weather – visited a good many people round about Westford, including MacDonald. Merchant, Dusary, who deals in tweeds, he has also got 2 shops in Lochmaddy. His retail price for tweed is 3/- per yard. if bought across the counter. I have so far not been able to discover what the merchants sell the tweed for to the larger shops in Glasgow etc. but someone stated that they sell exactly at the price they pay the people , i.e. 2/8 to 2/9 per yard and that they trust entirely to making a profit on the groceries etc they supply the people with. As soon as this tweed is paid for, the money is almost always handed straight back across the counter. The profit on tea, sugar, meal etc is supposed to be a tremendously high one.

Westford Inn

A good many of the women around here spin for private orders and get about 3/6d per yard. I imagine the vicinity of the Inn helps, and that "Anglers" order themselves tweeds.

Found out another maker of Horse Collars and door mats. Donald Eoghan MacInnes, Cladach Kirkibost, N. Uist, but he charges 6/- to 6/6d for collars and 5/- for mats , more than Roderick Macdonald of Cladach Baleshare who charged only 5/- for a collar.

MacInnes is to send some collars and mats to the St. Andrew's Sale.

Another crofter near here also makes the collars but has never sold any. His wife put their value at 4/- , they are rather well to do people and she spins only to supply her family.

Tuesday 20th August.

Bad storm of wind and Rain walked to Bayhead to call on Mr. Rose Schoolmaster (school summer holidays going on) found him in, and gleaned a good deal of information about the district and the people. He is not a Gaelic speaker as he comes from Elgin, but his daughter Maud aged 14 is – and knows most of the people very well – She is to show me the way to various places one day and meantime will explain about the "Register" and give some of the circulars to the girls and women whom she meets every day (twice) at the Fold , where about 50 of them come to milk the cows.

I was too wet after that to attempt any more visits.

Cattle were an important part of the daily life and in the summer months, the women and the young people left the village to go to the nearby sheilings or folds, which were areas of good grass land for cattle to graze on, often in a more remote area.

Wednesday 21st August.

Wrote letters all the morning. Heard that a Mrs Wilson from Lochmaddy (Lawyer's wife and a native of Berneray Island) had come to spend the day in the Inn, so saw her and asked her a good deal about the Island, heard there is much spinning and weaving, and agreed to go there with her on Monday 25th for the day, and wrote to the Rev Grant, Church of Scotland Manse, asking him to try to arrange a meeting of workers for me.

In the afternoon hired a dogcart and drove to the U.F. manse near Knockintorran, Bayhead, found Rev MacLeod and his wife both in, and got a number of names of spinners from them – he is an old man who has had 2 bad operations lately and is rather feeble – but very anxious to help about the Industries – She is Canadian and has no Gaelic but tries to get orders for women who knit etc –

In spite of a wet evening Mrs Macleod came out and took me to call at half a dozen houses, there are many knitters round there as well as spinners and weavers, some of the women practically support themselves by their work.

We went to see one very strange elderly "character" – Ann MacDougall – whose house is the nearest relation to a cave I have ever seen as a human habitation – it's entered by a long, low, narrow, dark passage with an elbow in it and a step downwards (one must advance head foremost) – just room for a wall bed (a family of cats and hens occupying it during the day) – the fire takes up all the space opposite – a tiny window with a seat under it occupies the right side of the room – and a small cupboard holding some books and plates and a teapot – with a spinning-wheel and stool standing in front of it – fills the left side – a line stretched from end to end near the ceiling festooned with half dry sheep's fleeces – completes the furnishing, add to this a thick fog of peat reek and a queer little old woman full of conversation and exchanging much repartee with the Minister to whom she now and then gave a hearty thump on the back –

She knits and crochets caps for Lady Dewar wife of the M.P. for Inverness. shire – – & is to send some and also a pair of socks to St.Andrews – all the things she knits are of homespun yarn – shawls, stockings, socks and caps – if she had some better patterns to copy I think she would improve – she is very anxious to get more work – but she and none of the people round here have any idea of the right shape for a sock or stocking – they all knit too tightly and the wool they make is too hard and coarse –

A weaver we went to see not far from Ann MacDougall's – one Angus John Ferguson – is also a Lobster-Fisher – & a very quick weaver – but says he can make more by the lobsters than the weaving – – his wife crochets white homespun shawls – but such an ugly openwork pattern – I fear they would not sell easily – I saw some really good shawls a day or two after near Westford, made by a girl who knows the Shetland patterns – and they are delightfully warm, soft and pretty – white homespun yarn single ply not twisted at all – but thicker than the Shetland. She is sending one to St. Andrews.

Shetland Shawls were sold throughout Scotland and in London at Home Industries Exhibitions. They were usually knitted in one or two ply and were treasured for their intricate lacy patterns. Skilled knitters in the Outer Islands could have seen them at Craft Sales in Inverness or elsewhere on the Mainland of Scotland.

Thursday 22nd August.

Lovely day – out all day – walking – picked up little Maud Rose at the schoolhouse and she took me to see a great many people – in the Paible District –.

In the townships of Balemore almost all the people spin their own wool – I saw some webs quite ready for the North Uist Cattle Show & Industry Exhibition at Westford on 30th August, & arranged that any that might not have been sold there should be sent to try their luck at St. Andrews – Angus MacDonald, Crofter, whose wife has two webs ready is to see about the packing & labelling & sending away of all the other webs in the township – He is a member of *An Comunn Gàidhealach* and was very interested when I told him about the Sale – There are people there (at Balemore) also who knit shawls and socks –

An Comunn Gàidhealach (literally The Gaelic Association), commonly known as *An Comunn* supports and promote the Scottish Gaelic Language, its culture and history at local, national and international levels. The society was founded in Oban in 1891 and is closely associated nowadays with the Mod. (Music Festival)

In, Mrs MacInnes, wife of the Sanitary Inspector, I discovered a really first rate Knitter – all sorts of elaborate stocking tops including one she called the "Running Rabbit" (really a running Stag) – Her mother Mrs MacDonald, has been teaching spinning for a year and a half in Islay – originally sent there by H.I. MacNab of Edinburgh – a large wholesale Firm who apparently does much in Tweeds, stockings etc – & – according to Mrs MacInnes – give good prices – she sells to him herself –

Stockings with fancy tops, either in a lacy pattern or two coloured parti-knitting were popular with Sportsmen, usually golfers or shooters, and there was a market for these hand knitted goods through the Scottish Home Industries, Craft Exhibitions and Commercial outlets from the late 19th Century onwards.

I believe if the Council could manage to give "Instruction" in knitting in North Uist – Mrs MacInnes would be a capital Teacher – (of course I said nothing about this to her) – She has won prizes for both stockings and webs of tweed at all the local shows – and won a prize at Oban last year for a web. (it was entered in her sisters' name "Mrs MacAuley, Hotel, Coll" but she secured the money)
her address is Mrs MacInnes, Creag Chas, Paible. N.Uist.

Friday 23rd August.
Visited a number of people in the townships of Cladach Kirkibost – several of whom have promised to send webs to St. Andrews.

Two sisters – Mary and Marion MacCorquodale – spin – weave – and knit the Shetland Shawls I wrote of –
Marion learnt to weave a year ago from Manderson 'Instructor' for the Crofters' Agency – She has always as much work as she can get through – makes about £1 a week and could make up to 30/- but she finds it too exhausting sitting all day at the loom – both sisters like making the shawls & aim to try making yarn for sale – I have given Mary an order to spin me a lb of the finest softest yarn she can do & have also ordered a lb from widow Mary Fraser of Clachan – as – so far – I have never seen any specimen of what they can do – They all acknowledge that what they make for themselves is too hard & coarse – but they say they can make it fine – It will be interesting to see the result of these two orders – the young woman's work and the old. I gave each a pattern of some very nice yarn made in Gairloch –

Maud Rose

Saturday 24th August.
Beautiful day – walked to Clachan to telephone to Grimsay about going there on Tuesday – & to find out what time the Ford would be open.

Saw Mr Ferguson Merchant, agent for the Crofters' Agency – he told me since I saw him he has come across a number of women who spin their own wool & has advised them to send tweeds etc to St.Andrews – & that he himself will see about the labelling packing, & sending off by steamer – he has been so wonderfully good about all this, as he is very busy with 2 shops and the Agency to look after – but – from all I hear he is really good to the people – in his private capacity as Merchant I mean –

I went again to see Widow Mary Fraser & ordered the lb of yarn – she and her daughter have just finished 2 webs for the Crofters' Agency – & now they have a couple of stone of their own wool which they would like to spin for a private order – if they can get one – at 3/6 a yard – & any colour that might be chosen by the person who orders it – it would make about 30 yards, but would not necessarily be all one colour –

Loch in North Uist

A croft and spinner in North Uist

In some of the crofts where spinning is going on, there are sons or daughters very ill with consumption, some very sad cases, but they also make one feel rather uncomfortable as to the ultimate destination of the tweed, and the effect on the Weavers who handle the wool spun in these houses, the latter certainly must run the greater risk, as after the tweed is "wauked" one suggests it would be more or less purified?

> When cloth had been woven and removed from the loom, a *luadh* session was planned. The waulking women, called *na mnathan luaidh* in Scots Gaelic, assembled at the house of the owner of the cloth after breakfast. The tweed, up to 70 yards long, was sewn together at the ends to make a continuous loop and then it was soaked in human urine, *fual* or *graith*, saved in each house for this sole purpose. The ammonia served to not only deepen and intensify the dye colors but also to remove the oils of melted livers of dogfish used to dress the wool. The spelling of 'wauking' varies.

On Tuesday 27th. I go to Grimsay Island for a couple of nights & on Thursday to Nunton Benbecula , to stay in a farmhouse, so if it is possible I may manage to return to Westford for the day and attend the Cattle Show with its Industry Stall.

This week have added over 50 names to the Register. Mrs MacKenzie, Factor's Wife, Balelone, sent me a list of a great many in the 3 townships near her house, these I have not been able to see at all.

Travelling Stationery and Postage Expenses from 18th Aug 1912.

	£	s	d
Carried forward from 18th Aug.	3	1	5½
Half-Ream writing paper.		1	3
Map of Uist and Barra, with postage		2	2
Dogcart Hire to Knockintorran, U.F. Manse		4	
Telegrams :– Rev. Grant, Berneray Island			6
Proprietor, Carnan Inn			6
Post-cards :– Hon. Sec. (2) 1d			
Mr MacElfrish (2) 1d			
Miss McLaren, Statimie, Inverness ½d			3½
Ferryman, Newton, N. Uist ½d			
Mr MacGillivray, Barra ½d			
Letters :– Local Convener St Andrews Sale 1d			
Mr MacElfrish 1d			
Schoolmaster, Tighary 1d			
Nicholsen, Grimsay 1d			
Postmaster, Sollus 1d			
Rev. Gillies, Clachan 1d			
Mrs MacKenzie, Sealpaig, Drs wife (2) 2d			
do do Balclone, Factor's wife (2) 2d			
Father MacMillan, Benbecula 1d			
Sir David Masson (his brother an authority on Gaelic - sent him the circular)		2	2.
Rev. Grant, Berneray. 1d			
Mrs Wilson, Lochmaddy 1d			
do Burnley-Campbell 1d			
Lady Marjory MacKenzie (Gairloch Knitting) 1d			
Mr MacGillivray, Barra 1d			
Mrs MacKenzie of Farr 1d			
Mr Macdonald, Milton. S. Uist 1d			
E. Tann, Stationer (sent cheque) 1d			
Miss MacLean, Nunton, Benbecula (2) 2d			
do MacKintosh, Creagorry 1d			
Hon. Sec. (4). 4d			
£	3 -	12	- 4.

Sunday 25th August to Sunday 1st September.
Creagorry. Benbecula.

(moved from Westford Inn, North Uist 27th Aug to Grimsay Island – and from there on 29th to Creagorry)

August. **Sunday 25th.**
Lovely day – wrote letters & diary.

Monday 26th. August.
Up at 6.a.m. – drove 15 miles to Newton Ferry – 4½ miles of it along the 'Cum' ttee Road" (Committee Road) which is full of holes – took 3 hours doing the drive. At the ferry met by Mrs Wilson from Lochmaddy and then set sail in a fishing smack to Berneray Island which is really part of Harris – – wind and tide both dead against us, and after many tacks we landed nearly 4 miles away from the point we had intended to make – near the schoolhouse – so had a long walk. Here met by the Established Minister's 2 girls, 15 and 16. – & a little further on by the Rev Grant himself – then a few other stray people joined the procession – half way to the school, as we were passing the U.F. Manse, Mr. Grant remembered he had forgotten to ask for the use of the school for the meeting which he had arranged for 12 o'clock – it was then 11.30 – so we all called on Mrs. Morrison at the Manse – he was away in Stornoway, – & – after some cakes and milk – secured the key & reached the school just in time.

The 2 agents of the Association were waiting for us – Mrs MacLeod of the Crofters Agency & Mr. Paterson of the Scottish Home Industries – over 100 people came & the benches were full to overflowing – Mr.Grant and myself both talked a little – & then everyone discussed the question of "no sale" at the present moment – and the advisability of trying something other than tweeds which they are doing so badly – No less than 6 weavers 4 women and 2 men said they would like to try weaving Clan tartans – a man and woman who looked carefully at the tartan skirt I was wearing – made in Harris – found 2 mistakes in the counting of the threads & were delighted with themselves –

A number of spinners agreed to try making yarn for sale & also to Knit stockings – they both took samples of my Gairloch Skein and want me to send them some well knitted – well shaped – stockings as patterns – the weavers would also like patterns of different clan tartans – I insisted on the fact that wherever possible home dyes must be used for the colours – the first tartans would almost require to be made to order? – at once the question arose of no wool of their own to try any new ideas with –

In a pamphlet written by the Duchess of Sutherland in 1901 she gives technical advice on vegetable dyes and lists them with their Botanical and Gaelic or Native name. Pamphlet reproduced in Appendix B.

I promised to put this difficulty before the Council in the hope that the associations will settle to encourage these new departments of the Industries – it was so interesting to find all the people anxious to improve matters & inclined to listen to new ideas – Many talked of the visit of the Duchess some years ago and would like to receive one also from 'Lady' Stewart MacKenzie –

After the talking was over I Kodaked the whole party in the School yard –

Spinners and weavers in the Isle of Berneray Harris

Mrs Wilson.
Rev. Grant
Mrs MacLeod. "C.A"
Paterson "SHI"
The Tram Man.

One of the old crofts in Berneray

But before that several women at the same moment asked me " how many inches are there in a yard"– 36 naturally I answered – " There!! The Agents are taking 37 to every yard that is in it" – much laughter – everybody talking together – including the 2 agents – & they explained how it is the custom when measuring a web of tweed which they are going to buy, that the agent who wields the yard-measure – at the end of each yard – places his thumb before moving on the measure to the next yard – the thumb uses up an inch they say – & this is what they have measured is a web of 37 yards – a whole yard is lost when the agent measures it – the agents declare this custom is followed in all shops and when told again the tweed is measured in this way – a few went so far as to say that not only is the thumb inserted broadside on – but – sometimes – lengthways also – thus swallowing up 3 inches every time! However this was treated as a good joke against the agents! –

After a 3 o'clock 'dinner' at the Grants Manse we walked back to our boat, but on the way paid a great many visits & saw many webs of tweed. I suggested that a number should be sent to St. Andrews & this was heartily agreed to, by all who had their own wool – also some Rugs – A few of the people weave out of hearth rugs , out of the coarsest bits of this wool – but they are rather expensive to make & it does not pay to sell one under 18/- or 20/- – & unfortunately they are rather like the jute things overseas being sold for about 5/- or 7/6.

Mrs MacDonald of the Post Office has a twig hand-loom which stands on a chair – and makes even smoother rugs – glorified door-mats – in 2 colours, with a fringe at each end – at 7/6 per yard – She was taught by some woman who came to the Island a year or two ago – sent – I think by the Crofters Agency – anyway it's splendid work for an invalid, but they look upon it more as 'family work' – although Mrs MacDonald said she could, if she sat at it, work a yard in a day – 7/6. She is to send one or two to St. Andrews – she is of course not an invalid – but it is work that might be done by a bed- ridden man or woman.

Only a very few of these people have their own wool – they don't seem to deal much in tweeds, with the merchants – mostly with both associations – I thought this trend was very good –

Berneray is a lovely little Island – the day was beautiful and no doubt it was looking its best – One district called Borve which had been a big 'Tack' and was cut up into Crofts – is known as the 'Golden Valley' from it's beautiful corn fields – all the new crofts in it have larger 2 storeyed homes with felt roofs – "Archie" a Tailor-Fisherman-Crofter combined – who has not got one – says they are far too large for the people who cannot afford to keep them up & have over built themselves – Half the men from there had gone over to the mainland of Harris to petition Lord Dunmore for more land – some Islands that used to go with the original farms – & these are the houses I visited as the woman was unable to attend the meeting, having no one at home to leave with the children.

A man from North Uist was at the meeting told me if I wanted a real good knitter his Mother was a 'specialist' at it & would I go and see her – across the ferry at the other side – finally he came and told me he had wired to her to say we were coming – and as he was going home that night, he got a lift in our boat and in the machine too for a couple of miles – we talked Glasgow and New York Trams, as he is in Trams at the former place – his mother Mrs Robertson is a really 'first rate' Knitter – she found me some of her stockings which were wet – hanging up to dry, so we could not quite tell as to shape, but as far as I could judge they seemed splendid – firm – soft – very well knitted & in all one colour patterns – she can do basket – cable and many others – besides ones she invented from looking at the plaits in her own hair! I believe she too would make an excellent 'Teacher' & I think if she could be ferried over to Berneray once or twice a week in the Winter, she might hold a class – her house is about 2 miles from the ferry, and she is young enough to make it all right – she is also a very good spinner –

We got back to Westport Inn about 9.30 that night – Mrs Wilson, her husband is sub commissioner in Lochmaddy (and always travelling about through the Islands) was most helpful all day – she knows everyone and said she will always be ready to help us in anyway she can about the Industries – she has only one small boy and with her husband away so much has a good deal of spare time –

Tuesday 27th. Aug.

Left Westford Inn in the morning and had the usual delays about getting the bill – and packing into the cart – Eoghan from Clachan came to fetch us – passing through Clachan saw Fergusson Crofters Agency – also called to say goodbye to the Gillies at the U.F.Manse – and onto more crofts – Then went on across the Ford (a mile ford) to Grimsay & had to hurry as the tide was coming in –

From Clachan I wired to Mrs MacDonald local convenor St. Andrews Sale to send labels, Rules to various people at Balemore, Knockintorran – & Cladach Kirkibost Townships – as they had never come and I had promised the people to let them get them in good time – of course that evening they did arrive – at best only a dozen labels and no Rules – the delay was caused by Mrs MacDonald having been away from home – but then she kindly said she would receive goods from the Outer Islands, right up to the days of the Sale – so that will make it much easier for the people –

Nicholson the merchant, whose home I was staying in – met me – & said he had arranged a meeting for me that evening in the school – had a long talk with him first & he abhorred the associations & said that at the end of the "Trade-Mark Law-Suit" the Lawyer Gentlemen had published for all the World to know that the 2 grand ladies were nothing but a firm of 30 gentlemen each – who had speculated their money in it to make a profit out of the poor people of the Islands"

No argument of mine – even the "John Bull"one – would induce him to alter his opinion – I went next day to the Hon. Sec. and reported this, and asked if some clear description of the case could not be printed and circulated in the Islands –

In 1906 the Harris Tweed Association was formed with the purpose of establishing a trademark to protect the authentic Harris Tweed industry and the livelihoods of the crofters in the Western Isles.

The Harris Tweed definition was registered in 1910 and inspectors were employed by the Association to authenticate and stamp, with the registered trademark, all genuine Harris Tweed. The mark consisted of an orb with a Maltese cross on the top of it, with the words Harris Tweed underneath the symbol. "Harris Tweed means a tweed, hand-spun, hand-woven and dyed by the crofters and cottars in the Outer Hebrides."

We had about a dozen people at the meeting who sell to the 2 merchants, Nicholson – & MacLean, Callan, Grimsay – very few have any wool of their own –

I think they sell to the merchants because its easier getting wool from them, bringing the finished web back again – instead of having to carry it across the ford – Clachan is the nearest Crofters Agency Depot – that is about 5 miles (but the Ford is a barrier always) and the Scottish Home Industries has, I <u>think</u> nothing nearer than Lochmaddy – which is about 13 miles distant including the Ford –

Weds. 28th. August.

Wrote all the morning – Walked some miles in the afternoon & paid a number of visits – no woods or paths in this Island , which is so intersected with Bays – which were <u>fords</u> when I started – & full of sea when I returned – & so rather puzzling to verify them again. – All the crofts on the outside edges of the Island – the middle is used for grazing only –

The houses here are miserably uncomfortable much smaller rooms than on the 'mainland' of North Uist & very dirty & untidy, most of them – less English here than in any place I have been to – the people all very nice – they require helping a good deal, I should say about the industries – from all I could discover Nicholson pays 2/7 a yard. & MacLean 2/8. – but the former told me he gives 2/8 too – only several people I asked said 2/7 – this means 3d. loss a yard than the lowest price the association gives – leaves very little room for profit to the poor worker. – Knitting might be encouraged here perhaps or yarn making –

There is a Crofter Cameron in some very isolated spot between the mainland of North Uist & Grimsay who makes the Horse Collars & who owns chains of the plaited Bent – I would not manage to go and see him but But I wrote & told him about St. Andrews & sent him a couple of labels in case he can send any things & enclosed a stamped envelope for him to let me know if he does – the chairs might be a good thing & he might teach other men – I wanted to see him but the rain came down in sheets that evening and I was already so wet & far from home I had to turn back –

I forgot to mention that at the meeting Nicholson said he would hand the woman the web they had spun for him back again & allow them to send them to St Andrews & make the profit – although the wool and webs were his & they would have to repay him – I said I would ask the Council as to this, he evidently had been trying to send in tweed on his account – If the Hon. Sec replies in the affirmative, I shall myself write the labels with the names of the women on them so that he can't stick on his own name –

The Island of Grimsay is made up of tidal sands, sea lochs, small islands and islets, and is four miles long and two miles wide, situated between Benbecula and North Uist. Grimsay was connected to neighbouring North Uist and Benbecula in 1960 with the opening of the North Ford Causeway.

Thurs. 29th. August.

Left Grimsay about 1 oclock

Had a long visit in the morning from one Angus Nicholson – brother of the merchant but older & quite different – a courteous old Hielandman – a sailor – is an agent for the steamer "Dunira Castle" – he brought me patterns of his wife's tweeds – one large web she has now ready (he had got the Steward on the Steamer to try & sell it to the tourists but with no result) & 3 other smaller pieces which are now in Glasgow in the custody of a firm "John Blackwood & Sons" 78 MacAlpine street. He had sent them there in exchange for goods & had already received 2 or 3 pairs of boots for his children – but – owing to the bad trade in tweeds just now – Morris B. have told him he may send them to St. Andrews if he likes – Angus suggested that a part of the money if they sold at the sale, should be sent straight to the Firm & the rest to him – but I said this would be too difficult to arrange & that he must pay back the Firms afterwards himself –

I work out 3 of the official labels with descriptions of the tweeds – and Angus' wife's name – then am to go to Morris Blackwood & they will send on the webs to the sale. – I wrote the labels myself in case of any hocus-pocus about the firm of Blackwood – & Angus went away very pleased.

John Blackwood & Son, were Wholesale & Retail tea merchants and grocers at 87 & 89 McAlpine Street Glasgow in 1912, the son Maurice who was dealing in tweed from the Outer Isles was at number 78.

We crossed the long Ford to Benbecula (3 miles – it's 4 from side to side, but we were already a mile on the way at Grimsay) in a cart & Nicholson met us on the other side in his spring-cart and drove us on the 7 miles to Creagorry – (the Nunton visit had to be postponed altogether, owing to the death of the Farmer's mother)

Crossing the Long "North Ford" to Benbecula.

Changing carts half way.

The Cairn is to mark the way.

Benbecula is quite a flat Island and simply honeycombed with lochs – many of the Crofts have good modern houses on them & look prosperous, the people are mainly all Roman Catholics –

Nicholson was most anxious to arrange meetings for me, but I told him so far I had settled nothing – I don't much trust the man – his reputation not a good one – this I had gathered from vague hints – nothing definite – his opening a 3rd. shop in Creagorry in opposition to the 2 old established ones is an unpopular thing – but I don't believe this would account for it all –

– Even yesterday a man was praising Stewart the weaver (a foreigner from Perth) & saying "he's as honest a man as any in this Island" – I asked "what about Nicholson? would you be saying the same of him?" – he looked at me & smiled, "it's not for any man to be saying things – but – he'll need it all" –

Friday 30th. August.

Wrote letters in the morning and waited in , expecting a call from Father MacMillan, –heard later that he is away for 2 or 3 days & returns on Saturday –

Visited the Post Office & a good many crofts in the near neighbourhood in the afternoon – the Benbecula people are very nice & anxious to discuss everything & prepared that the Council wants to help them – I gather that Father MacMillan has been telling them all about it –

Father John MacMillan, styled *Maighstir* Iain Dhonnchaidh. was born in Barra in 1880 and ordained as a priest in 1913. He worked firstly in Oban , then in Eigg and the Small Isles before being appointed to Benbecula in 1908. During his missionary work there he was regarded with deep affection by the people. Always travelling on foot he visited every family and took a deep interest in the Folklore and the traditions of his flock. He is remembered today by one of the catchiest 2/4 pipe marches ever written, composed by Norman MacDonald from Broadford, Skye.

They see that if tweeds don't sell – they must try something else – Every woman knits of course – but very few have done any for sale – the postmistress Mrs MacLeod is a good knitter & will send some stockings to St Andrews as a beginning – she has no time to spin, – but wants to earn money by knitting – Besides shooting-stockings I advised her to send a pair of Lady's black hose – she uses ordinary shop wool – At the "*Feill*" in Glasgow 5 years ago – our Ross-shire stall was besieged by people wanting to buy lady's black stockings & we had only a very few pairs – this fact I only recollected when seeing some Mrs MacLeod had made, and suddenly it occurred to me they might sell well –

Feill The Gaelic word translates as Fair, market or feast day, as in *Latha Feill Anndrais*, St. Andrew's Day, in this context it records an event run by the Highland Home Industries Board, where handmade goods from the Highlands and Islands were on Sale.

She told me of 2 other good knitters – One or two people came to see me in my rooms & ask about the Council & I have put up a notice that I will see anyone who likes to come between 7 & 8 any evening – (they now arrive at all times of the day! time is of no importance whatever in the Islands – except when crossing the Fords)

The timing of crossing the Ford was crucial , as it depended on whether the Tide was a High one (Spring) or a Low one (Neep). The Tides were different every day and every hour. The tides are also governed by the time of Year and the weather. Crossing the Ford was and is very dangerous, because of the channels and quicksands which were ever-changing.

Saturday 31st. August.

Went to the Scottish Home Industries Depot, which is open every Sat. morning – the agent MacMillan very civil & anxious to help – He is a sub agent – does no selling, just sends the web straight onto MacTavish at Lochmaddy –

He told me about one advertisement he saw in a paper the other day – a Firm at Carnwath – Lanarkshire – (the name he could not remember, but may be able to find it and send it to me), which sells "Genuine Harris, homespun, home-dyed, home-woven, at 3/11d per yard – MacMillan declares it is bound to [be] machine-spun anyway –

I saw another Harris advertisement today in the Daily Mail.

" Claytons' Red Harris Tweed Suits" " Every Harris Tweed sold here is endorsed with a Guarantee which is unimpeachable" " Gents suit – to measure 50/- 75/- is the price charged elsewhere"

"Clayton's 34 Fenchurch Street"

In the afternoon I hired a pony, and rode over to Nunton on the North West side of the Island – to see the weaver Stewart whom I have heard of as the one man who can weave Clan Tartans – it began to rain hard soon after I started & never ceased all night – my saddle twisted round & a passing crofter Angus MacPhie "piper" kindly tightened the girths & told me his wife is a good spinner & had heard I was soon to have a 'meeting' and they wanted to come – he was carting a load of whelks to London (via Creagorry!) –

At Nunton met Andrew MacKinnon, Lady Gordon-Cathcart's Gamekeeper – who put the pony in the stables & led the way to Stewarts' – the weaver comes from Perth & used to weave tartans 30 years ago in some mills in the South which had hand looms – & till two years ago when he made some for Mrs Burnley Campbell, had never been asked to make any – but he said he could with an ordinary machine make pieces as a pattern, – make for any clan. He has 2 looms in a charming tin house – apart from his dwelling house – his wife spins & dyes – one or two neighbours came in while we were talking & I got their names for the Register –

Mrs Burnley Campbell of Ormidale was a tireless worker in the movements to extend the use of the Gaelic Language and to spread abroad a knowledge of the culture of the Gaels. She studied and learnt the Gaelic Language as a young woman and had the distinction of being the only woman to have held the office of president of *An Comunn Gàidhealach*.

After that, MacKinnons wife gave me some tea in Nunton House – they are caretakers there as well – she spins too and has made £12. during the last year by selling to 'Anglers' in the Creagorry Hotel – quite a young woman with a little girl of 3 – He is a keen conservative & thinks Dr. MacKinnon will get in for Inverness-shire at the next election –

The rain and wind both awful & I had a horrible ride home – the pony constantly refusing to face it & preparing to turn and stand sideways & tuck her head between her forlegs[*sic*] – at last had to dismount & drag her along behind me the last two miles – met a man called MacKay who as soon as he saw me pulled a pattern of gray tweed out of his pocket and said his wife has just finished the web of 20 yards & what did I advise him to do with it – I said St. Andrews Sale – he seemed pleased at the idea & said it is her first web (a young couple evidently). They would like to come to the meeting at Torlum School.

I hope to have meetings on Monday & Tuesday evenings in Torlum & another school which is near Nunton – On Wednesday rode across the Ford to Carnan Inn, Iochar, South Uist.

The "South Ford" from the Benbecula side exactly opposite Carnan Inn South Uist.

Mounted postman wading across with His Majesty's Mails – almost before the Ford is "open"

Crofters crossing the Ford. They passed us as we were crossing too in a cart from Creagorry to Iochar.

Travelling & Postage Expenses from 25th to 31st August 1912.

		£	s	d
Hiring	Carried forward from 25th. August	3	12	4
	Dogcart from Westford inn to Newton Ferry 15 miles at 1/3 -		18	9
	Sailing-boat from Newton to Isle of Berneray & back		10	
	Half share of Cart Westford to Grimsay Island at 5/-		2	6
	do do do do Grimsay to Creagorry at 11/-		5	6
Telegrams	Mrs Macdonald, St Andrews, about labels (from Berneray)			7 ½
	do do do do do do (from Clachan)		1	4 ½
	Redirection of wire from Father Macmillan			6
Letters	Hon Sec. (2)			2
	Father MacMillan, Benbecula,			1
	Angus MacDonald, Crofter, Cladach Baleshare, about labels			1
	Mrs Wilson, Lochmaddy (2)			2
	Carnan Inn			1
	Mrs Macdonald, St Andrews			1
	Mary Stewart, Knitter, Clachan (sent her labels)			2
	Cameron, Chair-maker, Cnoc Cuidhean. (Sent labels)			2
	Mrs MacLeod, U.F. Manse Knockintorran			1
	Mrs Burnley Campbell			1
	Posting Circulars to President & Committee (11)			11
	£	5	13	8

This finishes the expenses for the first month.

The beginning of the Ford from the South Uist side

Crofters riding to the Cattle Market in Benbecula from South Uist.

An eighty-two span concrete bridge between Benbecula and South Uist was the first link in the chain of bridges, causeways and car ferries which brought the Western Isles together in the first half of the twentiethth Century. Completed in 1942, the single-lane bridge was about 800 metres in length and crossed by eight spans from Benbecula to the tiny Creagorry Island and then onto South Uist.

Constructed during the Second World War, its completion was related to the creation of the military airport on Benbecula as well as to the continuing problems of communication on the islands. It enabled the air base to be connected with the ferry port of Lochboisdale.

Sunday 1st to Sunday 8th. September 1912.
Carnan Inn. Iochar. South Uist.

(moved from Creagorry, Benbecula. to Carnan S. Uist on Weds. 4th. Sept.).

Sunday 1st. Sept.
Fine morning – poured with rain later – wrote diary.

Monday 2nd. September.
Beautiful day – settled to have a meeting in Torlum school tonight & in Balavanish School tomorrow – wired about it to Father MacMillan – he never answered – finally I met him in the afternoon on the road – & he made some excuse about the wire having been brought by some very slow old woman who took hours – but never mentioned the letter he must have received from me some days before – however he was full of enthusiasm about the Industries & begged me not to have the Torlum meeting until tomorrow at 4. & the Balivanich one immediately after between 6 & 7 o'clock – he said I might safely leave the arrangement in his hands & that he would come to both meetings & explain things to the people –

This completely settled, I did a good many visits the rest of the day – within walking distance.

Had been in the morning to see Nicholson, Merchant – he had such a nice wife whom I had not met before – he settled after all <u>not</u> to give the women back their tweeds for the St. Andrews sale – as he was afraid of not getting them again, if they were unsold & returned straight to the women, whom he found would at once sell them to some other Merchant!

He also read me a long " puff" about himself as a seller of pure Harris Tweed – this was in some small English Paper whose name I did not see – he sells through the advertisement he has in this paper at 3/6 a yard & is doing a large trade in this way he tells me.

The paragraph, which he read aloud to me with no stops, & a very Gaelic way of pronouncing most of the words, hinted that certain Charitable associations or organizations had not the monopoly of selling the tweeds – that others were equally anxious to help the poor people of the Islands & that in Alex Nicholson would be found such a helper. – At least this is the impression having it said left on my mind.

Tuesday 3rd. September.

A frightful storm of wind & rain – wrote letters all morning – in the afternoon drove, clad in oilskins, to Torlum school ...[piece torn out of book !]

... good talk about the Industries – tweed – knitting & yarn making – 2 women had pieces of tweed ready, & agreed to send them to St. Andrews, & the others promised to make some yarn for the sale.

No message came from Father Macmillan, however I drove on to Balivanich School – & found the same thing there – school shut – the mistress away (Miss Fife), but the father, mother, & sisters who were staying there opened it for me, & about a dozen people, brought by Alex Stewart the weaver & his wife who had seen me pass – & by Mrs. Angus MacPhie "piper" who knew the meeting was to be, as he was in our house the evening before & the landlady had told him –

Stewart was most useful in explaining everything to the women & so was Neil Mackintosh, our landlady's brother who had driven us, he is a Lovat Scout trooper & full of energy!

> The Lovat Scouts was a British Army unit, formed by the 14th Lord Lovat during the Second Boer War. Its soldiers were recruited from ghillies, shepherds and stalkers in the Highlands of Scotland, whose skills in stalking in rough ground made them excellent intelligence gatherers.
>
> In 1902 the unit was reformed into two regiments, the 1st and 2nd Lovat Scouts, including a sharpshooter unit.

– Stewart will pack & label the St.Andrew's parcel from all the women who were at this meeting.

Had a long drive home without lamps and in the dark – ... [part torn out of book].. – he is always composing Gaelic songs & music & is a regular attendant every year at the "Mod" – when I knew him in the Isle of Eigg he was all right.

Wednesday 4th September.

Another day of storms – the Ford is so bad at first they said we shouldn't be able to get across at all – still – we started about 4. & our cart managed it safely although the water was up to the top of the wheels & the horse only just not swimming – after we had landed at the Carnan side of South Uist, crowds of men, women, horses & cattle streamed across the Ford to Benbecula for the Market next day – the people all sitting down just on the rocks taking off their shoes & stockings, rolling up their trousers & kilting their petticoats – ponies & calves had to swim – it was a most picturesque sight –

Going to Market via the Ford.

Carnan is in the extreme north of the Island of South Uist – The Inn is also the Post Office & a Merchants' (Temperance Inn) & is kept by Mr and Mrs. MacLean, he is a brother of MacLean, Merchant, Carinish, N. Uist.

Thursday 5th Sept

More storms – all these days the mails have been most erratic, sometimes the letters via Lochmaddy couldn't get across the North Ford to Benbecula – & then those via Lochboisdale got blocked at the South Ford which is over at Creagorry – in these storms the Fords become so deep & the current so strong it's dangerous for the Riding Postman when the tide is out and when it's in, a sailing boat would get swamped.

The power of the tidal waves and the sea at the South Ford, is very particular to this part of the world. There is a wave climate and storm surges from the Atlantic create life threatening conditions. Many people lost their lives crossing the Ford, the most recent tragedy was in January 2005.

Today I found it impossible to walk any distance, one got dead tired in half a mile – struggling against the wind & rain – I have never met anything like it in the Mainland & in spite of oilskins the rain penetrates somehow –

Paid 4 calls – very miserable houses, 2 weavers & 2 spinners – most depressing listless people as if there was some sort of a blight over them – but it may have been the weather.

Friday 6th Sept.

Storms – with fine intervals, got through a good many letters including a long one to the Hon. Sec.

In the evening visited 2 very cheery houses and came home with a different impression of the South Uist character!

A Mrs MacPherson who spins her own wool makes lovely tweed – so soft and firm –

Saturday 7th Sept.

Wind gone down – but it rained without a single break all day – I didn't go out – having got rather a chill from the other wettings and cold winds.

Labels arrived from St.Andrews – did tags & sent off a number to people in North Uist & Benbecula – & wrote letters explaining about them.

Mrs. MacLean our landlady knows a great deal about spinning, weaving, knitting, dyeing & wool, and she has been telling me a lot about it – she also knows all the workers in this neighbourhood.

Several people lately have complained to me that the Scottish Home Industries pays as low as 2/5 & 2/6 per yard & sells at 5/9. – so I've written to ask MacTavish S.H.I. Depot. Lochmaddy as to this – as one can't say anything one way or the other unless one knows the correct figures.

My impression is that the day I saw MacTavish he told me they pay from 2/10 to 3/- a yard & sell at 3/6 & 4/-.

I stay at Carnan till Friday 13th. when I start for St. Andrews via Oban, in the Steamer "*Hebrides*".

Travelling – Stationery – Postage Expenses
Saturday 1st. to Saturday 8th. September 1912.

		£	s	d
	Carried forward, month of August	5	13	8
Hiring	Dogcart to Torlum & Balivanich Schools		6	
	Pony to ride while at Creagorry		3	
	Half-share of Cart, Creagorry to Carnan, across the South Ford at 4/6.		2	3
Stationery	Envelopes			4
	200 coloured cards for Index at 1/- per 100, postage 3d.		2	3
Postage	Telegrams. Reply paid to Father MacMillan		1	7
	Ferguson, Daliburgh, South Uist	6		
	Post. card. Carnan Inn			½
	Letters. Hon. Sec. (3)			3
	Mr MacElgnish			1
	Father Walker, South Uist			1
	Rev. Boyd. Ch. of Scotland Manse. South Uist			1
	Alex. Stewart, Weaver, Nunton, Benbecula (labels)			1
	MacTavish, S.H.I. Depot. Lochmaddy			1
	Roderick MacKenzie (about dyes)			1
	Miss Molloy (sold her homespun) (2)			2
	Mrs. Eoghan Maclellan, Clachan. N. Uist			1
	Mrs. Robertson, Newton Ferry. N. Uist			1
	Maud Rose. Schoolhouse. Bayhead. N.U.			1
	Mrs. MacInnes, Creag Chastan, Paible. N.U.			1
	Mrs. MacLeod, Post Office. Creagorry. Benbecula			1
	Emily Macdonald. Linaclate Muir. Benbecula			1
	Widow Ferguson. Linaclate. Creagorry do			1
	Margaret MacDonald. Griminish. Benbecula			1
	Mrs. A. Mac Cormick. Harlat. do			1
	Mrs Eoghan MacDonald. Linaclate Muir do			1
	£	6	11	4 ½

Carried forward	6	11	4 ½
Letters continued.			
Mrs MacKay. Torlum. Benbecula			1
Miss MacKintosh. Merchant. Creagorry			1
Mrs Donald MacPherson. "R.S." Torlum			1
Kate MacDonald. Penmaenach. Torlum			1
Seonaid MacMillan. Benbecula			1
Maggie Vicar. Strome. Creagorry			1
Kate MacMillan. Hacklet. Benbecula			1
Widow Neil Wilson. Griminish. do			1
Mrs. John Wilson. Benbecula			1
Margaret MacDonald. Griminish do			1
£	6	12	2 ½

Neil MacKintosh & MacSween the "Ground Officer" starting home across the Ford to Creagorry – having left us at Carnan Inn.

Off to Market over the Ford.

Sunday 8th. to Sunday 15th. September.
Written at Oban.
(sailed from Loch Carnan, South Uist. on Fri. 13th.
arrived Oban mid-night on Sat 14th.)

Sun 8th. Very wet – wrote diary.

Monday 9th September.
Another cold wet day – drove to Ard-Kenneth, Eochar, to call on Father Walker – he was very civil – had already been telling his people they must take my advice about the Home Industries – and make the things I might suggest –

I paid a number of calls in his neighbourhood & found everyone ready to talk about things – secured some nice webs of tweed for St. Andrews –

Tuesday 10th September
Did an 8 mile walk with Mrs MacLean, my landlady at the Carnan Inn – out for 6 hours & visited over a dozen crofts, chiefly in the Gerinish District – Gerinish is another of the big "Tacks" which has been split up into Crofts by the Congested Districts Board – about 5 years ago – & is now a prosperous looking Township – all have good houses – but the crofts are only of 20. acres arable & the "Machairs" for grazing – they pay £5. rent and £5. interest on the money advanced by the board to build the houses – Mrs. MacLean declares the holdings are not large enough & that in a few years the people will be as badly off as they were before –.

The Congested Districts Board was set up in 1897. The purpose of the Board was to offer practical help to those living in the Crofting Counties: help to establish fisheries and new piers, and to provide weaving equipment. Crucially, it was given the power to purchase farms from landowners to be broken up into crofts (smallholdings).

In 1904 the Secretary of State for Scotland submitted to Lady Cathcart a report he had received on the state of society in South Uist. It mentioned that there were about 197 cases of persons who were desirous of getting land, and in the Under-Secretary's memorandum it was stated that if about one-fourth of these could be accommodated he thought the situation could be sufficiently dealt with. Lady Cathcart, gave up two farms—one named Kilbride and the other Gerinish—and handed them over to the Congested Districts Board for the purpose of making small holdings.

I saw some very good tweeds and also a few knitted things – met two women who say they can "lift" knitting directions out of a book – & would like to try some new things – one had made rather a good "Sweater" in white homespun yarn to send to her husband in Canada – however I commandeered it & she was to start a new one for her husband directly – I am taking it to St. Andrews priced at 10/6. as there is so much wool in it besides the work.

Saw the weaver who had woven the MacDonald Tartan plaid spun by the mother of Mrs Ferguson, Clachan, North Uist – which was so beautifully made – this weaver is quite a young woman with small tiny children – She thinks she could do a tartan again – but is not quite sure – as the old woman helped her in setting it up – I think if possible it would be a good thing to get her an order – so that she can get the old woman, who is still alive but no longer does much, to come over & help her to start it –

It's one of the few Protestant Houses we went to and met the Rev. Boyd. of the Church of Scotland – also calling – rather lucky meeting him as I had already written to him – he and I sat in the "Room", with the company also of a hen! & had a "cup of tea in the hand" – while our hostess & Mrs Maclean had theirs much more comfortably by the hot peats in the kitchen –

– The Rev Boyd is a young man – very well groomed – is supposed to take very much interest in his flock – who are a mere handful in this Island of Catholics & a few United Frees besides. – however he appeared quite interested in all I told him – & next day a very good web of tweed arrived from a Mrs MacRury who lives quite near his manse & a long way from Carnan – He also promised to tell the people I would come & see them early in October –

The woman who wove the tartan on her loom makes floor rugs or bed-covers as well.

It was a lovely walk & we saw the most beautiful bit of the country I have seen yet in the Outer Isles – the whole extent of Loch Bee – backed by Ben More – at the foot of which is Prince Charlies' cave –

Charles Edward Stuart, known as 'Bonnie Prince Charlie' or 'the Young Pretender', was born in 1720. He was the grandson of King James VII of Scotland and II of England, and he believed – along with his Jacobite followers – that the British throne was his birthright.

– The Loch is inhabited by wild swans – over a thousand they say – partly native and partly visitors from Norway – I counted over a hundred floating in the water with their heads to the breeze – as I walked along the causeway road which goes right across the Loch – this road too is interesting – to get from the North of the Island to the South – people used to be obliged to walk right round the loch, – a long way – but in the year of the Potato famine – thirty years ago or so – lady Gordon Cathcarts' father, the proprietor fed the whole island – & made the men pay in work – this road was the result and it has been a boon to them ever since –

A third of the population of the Highlands emigrated as a result of the potato famine. Relief money ran out in 1850 and the burden of providing for the population fell back on the landlords. There was also a wave of compulsory clearances as landowners feared they might become a financial burden. People were bundled onto ships and sent to Nova Scotia, while sheep took their place in an empty landscape. The stories from these evictions and deportations after the potato famine in 1850, are extremely chilling and first hand Oral accounts from S. Uist give details of brutal practices towards human beings and the burning of their houses.

At one end of the new Township of Gerinish is a most palatial looking school like a Town- Hall! – erected by an extravagant board to accomodate 20 children!

Gerinish school was opened in 1909. The School Board had pressed on with the building of new schools in Uist meeting their obligation under the Education Act. These new schools were in the newly settled areas. The problem was who was going to pay for them?

The cost of the new schools was to be borne by the rates. This meant that the parish council would have to levy a rate that was far in excess of anything that had existed in the past and was by far the highest in Scotland. The matter went to the Court of Session. The Court decided that that the Parish Council was legally obliged to collect the rates. The Parish Council then resigned 'en bloc'. The Clerk to the Parish Council, R. MacMillan, living in Gerinish, issued rates notices including one to Lady Gordon Cathcart in which he threatened to *poind* her goods if she did not pay. She appealed to the Court of Session. The Court found in favour of MacMillan.

All the people seemed so fond of Mrs. MacLean, & she had a bag of sweeties with her, some of which were poured into the hands of every child we came across – She was educated at the School Lady Gordon Cathcart used to have for the girls of the Island, – & the training she received there seems to have left a life-long impression on her – a pity there is nothing of the same sort now-a-days, they all drift to Glasgow where they mostly lose their health – & learn too, to despise spinning & knitting –

The MacLean family is one of the old fashioned kind – the father a stern old U.F. Churchman – I witnessed a delightful scene by accident one day in his shop (at the moment I was hatless, behind the counter writing out a wire) in burst four ladies – English Shooting Tenants from the Lodge 8 miles off –
"We want to buy some sweeties" "I'm not keeping them at all" said Allan – groans of disappointment from the four – "and will you be wishing to know why I am not keeping them?" said he after a short pause – " Well, it is this way, they will be bad for my childrens teeth & I will not be allowing temptation in their way" – gasps of surprise from the shooting tenants "But are not all your children grown up?" with a glance from his long white beard to me behind the counter –

"Yes, Yes –" very testily – & bored by the subject – which he considered closed –

"But it will be all the same"

They bought 2 picture postcards & took a pattern of tweed – in the course of which they and I exchanged several remarks in my new role as daughter of the shop – then Allan – relenting a little, told them they could get "sweeties in plenty" in Creagorry across the Ford – They were jubilant, till I remarked kindly how much they would enjoy the wade! – whereupon they fled from the scene without saying goodbye or thank you!

Weds. 11th September

Stormy again – Held a sort of reception in the Inn – men & women coming all day with tweeds & yarn – each one stayed a good half hour – James Mackay from Torlum, Benbecula, the same man who stopped me the day I was riding home from Nunton, rode across the Ford to ask about his wife's Web. – as he was afraid it might be too late if they sent it by the *Hebrides* & goods train – so I told him to bring it over to Carnan & it could travel with me like the others from there – so he brought it next day, a very good piece – dark gray – beautifully spun and woven, but rather an uninteresting colour. – they are a family of 5 brothers who have always been very good to their old mother – & this one is the first to marry. He priced the tweed at 4/- per yd. but James said whatever happened (however much it had to be reduced) it must not come back – as it would be so disappointing & unlucky too – her first web.

Thursday 12th Sept.

Very busy all day helped by Mrs Maclean, labelling , measuring – & making a list of all the stuff for St. Andrews and packed up the following: –

18. webs of tweed
3. of drugget
1, Floor – Rug –
1, Horse. Collar –

all this took a long time –

Hamish Mackay.
Riding across the Ford with his wife's first web of Tweed.

Had a visit from Mr MacLean from Nunton Farm, Benbecula, & Mrs Wilson (Sub. Commissioners Board of Agriculture) the husband of this Mrs Wilson who came to Berneray with me – both seemed much interested in the Industries – especially Mr Wilson – he is very anxious a lace-making class should be started – his great idea is to keep the best of the young girls from going off to Glasgow – as he wants them to marry the Crofters who are getting the new Holdings – so he thinks if they had some work other than Tweed-making – more refined kind of work – they might be induced to stay at home more –

While the Crofting Act of 1886 was a great step forward, giving security of tenure, fair rent, the right to dispose of the tenancy, and the right to compensation for improvements, there were still many problems to be addressed, principal amongst which was the problem of overcrowding and the demand for the farms to be broken up into crofts.

I talked afterwards to Mrs MacLean about this – as to whether there would be any chance of any of the girls taking to it – & she thinks with a few from Benbecula & some from Carnan a class might be started – her own 2 daughters would like it very much – also the Doctors daughter – I believe if it then started that she & her daughter would be the people to keep it going & mange it well – they are full of energy & have a good deal of influence among their neighbours – The Benbecula girls could easily cross the Ford – to the class – I promised to put the idea before the Council – but of course before arranging anything, one would have to find out if enough girls could be got together to make it worthwhile –

The MacLeans second daughter, Katie, has had such a sad thing happen to her just lately – a bicycle accident – her foot was injured – blood poisoning set in – & it had to be amputated – is not yet quite healed – poor girl – she was a cook and very fond of her work – had been trained at a Technical School in Aberdeen – but now will never be able to go on with it – as she couldn't manage so much standing – so it would be a splendid thing for her if she could get some new interest in life – such as lace making – then perhaps teaching others – but she would not be strong enough to go away from home to learn – I have been wondering whether Lace-making & knitting might not be combined, with her as a sort of Supervisor? I believe a great deal might be made by knitting all sorts of things besides socks & stockings – gloves, – "sports coats" – "sweaters" & other things. – If there is any chance of being able to arrange this plan, I could ride out to Carnan from Millers Farm when I return to South Uist – I don't suppose it will do to start anything now till the end of January when the days grow longer – at least nothing to do with lace – but a few preliminaries might be settled –

By 1912 various publications giving instructions for home knitting had been published in Britain and the United States of America. Included were two coloured parti-knitting patterns for Fancy patterned Golf socks and Tops and Muffatees.

Friday 13th September.

Pouring with rain – SS. *Hebrides* reported arriving about 1. o'clock in Lochcarnan four miles from the Inn – drove over there in enough time and had five hours to wait – very wet and cold – sheltered in Farquhar MacMillans Croft – there were 20 people in the kitchen by the fire – & in the "Room" was my cousin & myself & father Walkers wife (a cook on her way back to her place in England) without a fire – very stuffy cold – after four hours of the Cooks Conversations & maddening nostalgia, I simply had to go for a walk – & got wetter still – mercifully soon after 5. the *Hebrides* came into sight – & we all clambered down the rocks into the small boats and rowed out to meet her – The reason she was so late was owing to a phenomenally low tide, which happens once in 3 years & so she could not get into the Loch – but had to go on to Loch Skipport – further South, & then return to fetch us – We were due in Loch Boisdale in another 2 hours but as a matter of fact took exactly 14 – (arrived there at 7. next morning) – as we ran straight into a fog – and lost our bearings – wandering about all night – sometimes mooring for 10 minutes – then the engines stopping – fog-bell clanging all the time.

Saturday 14th September.

After Loch Boisdale we put in to Castlebay in the Isle of Barra. – & having to get in some cargo – spent a few hours there – so were all to land & look around – such a dear little place – very hilly – there is a ruined Castle on a wee Island in the harbour – hence the name.

Most of the women were just back from the East Coast Fishing – but some had already started off to England – (Yarmouth & other Places) – they are all "Fishgutters" –. I saw the complete outfits of oilskins they wear to work in – skirt & apron combined & a short jacket – leather Wellington boots – they get very good pay, but it must be disgusting work –

> After a slump in the Herring Industry in the 1880s agents took over the business and the status of a common fisherman was transformed into that of a wageworker. Under these circumstances the role of the female fish workers as breadwinners of the family became important. Permanent migration and emigration started from the Isles when the Russian herring market was lost.

The Purser strongly advised me not to take a return ticket on the *Hebrides* on Tues. 24th. as I meant to do – as he said they might be 3 nights on the way to Barra – & also might come in for very bad weather – & instead of going straight to Barra from Oban she goes North along the West Coast of Skye – via Tarbert & Lochmaddy & other places – – but he said MacBraynes' Mail boats run from Oban at 6.a.m. 3 times a week & arrive Castlebay the same evening – so I settled to do this – (it means a single ticket each way as they are different pairs of Steamers).

In addition to steamers and ferries, there are early references to the effects of extreme weather on shipping.

In January 1873 six men were lost when their boat encountered a storm in the Minch, a strait separating the north-west Highlands and the northern Inner Hebrides from Lewis and Harris in the Outer Hebrides. (*The Scotsman*, 21 January 1873).

We called at Tiree – Coll – & Tobermory – the first 2 – fascinating looking Islands – but there was no time to land – Arrived Oban about midnight – & heard that no trains leave till Monday morning – so I shall be stuck here for 2 nights & can't reach St. Andrews till mid-day on Monday.

The tweeds went on to Glasgow by the *Hebrides* – & then by passenger train to St A. so I hope they will get there by Mon. night.

Found a long letter awaiting me from the Hon. Sec. telling me about the Councils meeting here on 9th. a few days ago.

This is another picture of the Grogorry Flock at the South Ford.

"South" Mail Iochar to Benbecula. (The South mail is important & has a machine to carry her. The North mail has only a mounted Postman).

Isle of Tiree (from SS. *Hebrides*)

Travelling – Stationery – Postage Expenses.
from Sunday 8th. to Sunday 15th. Sept. 1912.

	Carried forward.	6	12.	2 ½
Hiring.	Dogcart to Eochar from Carnan Inn (call on Priest)		5.	
	Dogcart to Lochcarnan (to catch Steamer, self & luggage).		5.	6.
Steamer.	Lochcarnan to Oban – single fare		15.	
	porter Oban – mid-night		1.	
Stationery.	Labels for tweeds. (extra ones required so I had to use plain ones & write them out).			6.
Telegrams.	St Andrews – for more sale labels			6.
	St Andrews – about teamer delasys (twice)		1.	
	Post master Lochboisdale (had been making a muddle about forwarding letters).			6.
Postage.	Sending parcels of yar & stockings to the sale			2.
Letters.	Macdonald. Farmer. Milton. S. Uist			1.
	Hon. Sec. (Diary – lost week)			1.
	MacGillivray. Eoligarry. Barra.			1.
	MacTavish. Scottish Home Industreis. Lochmaddy.			1.
	Post master Lochmaddy			1.
		8.	3.	7 ½

Carnan Inn

Iochar

South Uist.

Sunday 15th to Sunday 29th September 1912.

(Oban - St. Andrews - Aviemore - Isle of Barra).

Sunday 15th Sept At the Station Hotel Oban – wrote diary –

Monday 16th Sept.

Left Oban 6.a.m. train – Arrived St Andrews about 1. o'clock.
Met Mrs Burnley-Campbell – Also met Mrs MacDonald, Local Convenor of the *Comunn Gàidhealach* Industries sale –
Spent the rest of the day till after 9.p.m. in the Volunteer Hall – helping to arrange & classify things for the Sale.

> From the *Dundee Courier* 18 September 1912:
> A 3 day sale of work at the Volunteer Hall to help the work of the Highland Home Industries Association. Opened on 17 September by Lady Ninian Crichton Stuart who said "she had great sympathy with what was known as the Celtic revival, and by encouraging these home industries which had come down to them from the past they were keeping alive the traditions of their forefathers, thus preserving national sentiment. They were also assisting these Highland craftsmen to better their meagre livelihood (applause)." She was thanked by Mrs Burnley-Campbell, Glasgow. There was a good display of Argyllshire tweeds, Harris Tweeds, Sutherland home spuns, baskets, etc.

Tuesday 17th Sept.

Busy with the Tweeds all this morning – Then Sale was opened at 2.15. by Lady Ninian Crichton Stuart, who was introduced by the Bishop of St Andrews.

> Lady Ninian Crichton Stuart of the House of Falkland,was one of many benefactors of the Home Industries. Today the Estate of Falkland is run as a Centre for Stewardship, sharing the wealth of land and environmental assets with the Community of Fife and the rest of Scotland.

As there was not enough people to sell, I joined in the work all three days – and spent most of my time at the stocking & yarn stall – besides sometimes spinning for half an hour or so when anyone wanted to see how it was done – and also persuading people to buy or rather give orders for "Drugget" – In this I was far more successful than I had hoped – booked 10 or 11 orders for different colours & also an order for a homespun MacDonald tartan Plaid – About £150. made.

Drugget was the most commonly worn woven fabric in Scotland, as a working skirt material up until the first quarter of the 20th. century. It was usually a mixture of wool and linen, but after cotton became readily available, that was often used as the warp. The 'strippet' petticoat in Folksongs describes the drugget skirt. It is easily recognisable in traditional dress and national costumes as it is a striped closely woven, coarse, durable fabric.

Weds. 18th. Sept.

Second day of the Sale – Not so many people came but about £70. made.

Thurs. 19th. Sept.

Last day of the Sale – In the evening a good many working mens' wives came in & bought socks and yarn also flowers & vegetables – Made about £48.

Receipts from the whole sale – are – roughly : –

Sold by Mrs Macdonald beforehand	£100
First day	150
Second day	70
Third day	48
Bought by Council for Canada	60.
	£428.

The Highland Home Industries Sales were run with precision, indicated here by the dress code expected.

The costume of the Stall holders was prescribed thus: For the Island Stall, Dress - stall holders: black or white with hat, sash or rosette of own tartan with clan badge; Assistants: black or white with hat and badge or rosette of tartan of President or Convenors. The convenors represented Jura, Mull, Lewis, North Uist and Bute.

Fri 20th Sep.

A very busy day finishing off all the work of the 3 days – writing down what was left – choosing (& noting down all parti: colours of them) the Webs for Winnipeg & Canada – Sat up till 2.a.m. making lists & calculating the prices etc. The Council voted £60. to be spent on this.

13. Webs chosen for Winnipeg.

Yards	at.	Name & Address of the Worker	£	s.	d.
16 ½	5/-	Johan Sutherland. Burnside. Rogart. Sutherland.	4.	2.	6.
11	4/6.	Mrs. MacDonald. Ulna Schoolhouse. Tayvallich Lochgilphead. Argyll.	2.	9.	6.
13 ½	4/6.	W. Macdonald Semple. Beulah Villa. Fort Augustus Inverness-shire.	3.		9.
9.	4/6.	Mrs. Donald Ross. Lairg. Sutherland.	2.		6.
12 ⅝	4/6.	Widow Hugh Murray. Blairich. Rogart. Sutherland	2.	16.	9¾
9 ½	4/6.	Margann Murray. Barnhill. Rogart. Sutherland.	2.	2.	9.
12	4/6.	Mrs Angus Nicholson. Kallan. Grimsay Isle. North Uist.	2.	14.	
16 ½	4/6.	Maria MacKay. Achnagarrin . Rogart. Sutherland.	3.	14.	3.
8	4/6.	Mrs Lachlan Macdonald. Carnan. Iochar. S. Uist	1.	16.	
8¾	4/6.	Mrs. Donald Ross. Tornich. Lairg. Sutherland.	1.	15.	4 ½
6 ½	4/6.	Mrs John MacKinnon. Clachan. North Uist.	1.	9.	3.
6¾	5/-	Mrs. Peter MacLeod. Baledubh. Iochar. S. Uist.	1.	13.	9.
8 ½	5/6.	George MacIver. Strath Conon. Muir of Ord. Ross-shire	2.	2.	6.
			31	17.	11¼

Six Webs for Canada, other than Winnipeg

Yards	at.	Name & Address of the Worker	£	s.	d.
23	4/6.	Mrs R. Maclennan. Cuidinich. Obbe. South Harris.	5.	3.	6.
10	4/6.	Morag Paterson. Borve. Isle of Berneray. N. Uist	2.	5.	
16	5/-	Mrs. James MacKay. Torlum. Benbecula.	4.		
53 ½	4/6.	Kenneth MacLeod. 6. Calbort. Loche. Stornoway. Lewis.	12.		9.
8 ½	4/6.	Mrs. John MacLean. Balemore. Lochmaddy. N. Uist	1.	18.	3.
10	4/6.	Mrs. R. MacLeod. Quay. Isle of Berneray. North Uist.	2.	5.	
			28.	2.	6.
		Winnipeg : –	31.	17.	11¼
		Canada : –	28	2.	6.
			60.	0.	5¼

Things left un-sold – that may go to
Edinburgh for a small Sale in Dec.

50 webs of Tweed. (8 "Reserved" for Canada).
2. plaids or Railway rugs. ("Reserved" for Canada).
38. pairs stockings.
11. pairs socks.
8. Bundles Yarn – 3 of Thread & 1. Metal Candlestick
(these last Mrs Stewart. Cupar Fife. is trying to sell privately).

In 1903, exhibitions of French Canadian handwoven goods, inspired farmer's wives in Montreal and a new organisation The Society of Arts and Crafts of Canada was formed in Ontario. Two exhibits sent to London resulted in Princess Louise, Duchess of Argyle, ordering suits of Canadian homespun for herself and her husband. At the same time the Handicrafts Committee were in touch with the Duchess of Sutherland about her work for the Scottish Home Industries.

Sat 21st. Sept.

Busy in the hall all the morning with Mrs MacDonald– saw that the things left over which are eventually to go to Edinburgh were safely stored with the Canadian Consignment in a small room adjoining the hall till Tuesday when Mrs MacDonald is to see them put into the Warehouse of MacGregor upholsterer – they are to be insured –
Left St Andrews at 2.p.m. and arrived that evening at Aviemore.

The Sale. (Notes on it)

Tweeds.

It was a great success – especially from the tweed point of view – there was a very family representative show of these from the Highlands & Islands – although the fact of the Highland Home Industries at Inverness taking place at the same moment may have affected it a little –
There was a large quantity of Islay Tweeds very pretty, most of them – but there remains a doubt as to whether some of it is not partly made by machining? –
The Sutherland workers tweed was by far the finest & softest tweed & also the best colours –

Plaids & Tartan

There were several very good Rugs & Plaids – two rolls of Tartan – one double width of the Black Watch,

– some of this sold – & the other MacKenzie none of this sold but it would have been better to have sent it to Inverness! St. Andrews would not naturally be a good place in which to sell tartans –

Stockings

The stockings were disappointing – not half enough sent in & all the really well knitted well shaped ones were bought up the first day – any number more might have been sold had they been there – as it was a good many pairs of badly shaped ones, & ones with brilliant tops were left unsold – the stockings came practically from 2 districts – i.e. Gairloch in Ross-shire and Oban. (many sent on from the Oban Industries).

Socks.

Fingering socks sold well but not the Homespun ones.

Yarn.

Good Homespun yarn also found ready purchasers – most of this was from the Outer Isles, the result of my many talks on the subject – some of it really good & some too hard & thick – all that was left over I entrusted to the care of Mrs Stewart, Rumgally House. Cupar Fife, who is to try & sell it among her friends (she bought large quantities of it herself) if this is successful it will go to Edinburgh with the other things.

Rumgally House, sometimes called Rumgay or, in old writings, Rathmatgallum, is a fourteenth Century hunting lodge set in twenty-five acres. In 1528 it formed part of the extensive barony of Strathmiglo.

Wicker-Work.

The Wicker work was also disappointing – all from Skye except a horse collar which came from South Uist & won first prize – to my mind the baskets were too fanciful & useless – except the Waste-paper ones which were all right. The 'Judges' were Mr. MacKenzie, Earlshall, whom I talked to said it was such a pity they had nothing characteristically Celtic in their design – & that if not that they should have been stronger & more useful –

Earlshall was formerly part of the estate of the Earls of Fife. Mr MacKenzie was interested in the Arts & Crafts movement and, with his great friend William Burrell, encouraged Lorimer. (Sir Robert Stodart Lorimer, Architect). Amongst other talents, MacKenzie was a great expert on restoring antique tapestries.

There were various work-baskets – small tea-trays with wooden bottoms, mainly the rims of wicker-work – Knife trays of the same kind – a daffodil basket was better but hardly strong enough either – The wicker-furniture as far as I saw consisted of a flimsy two- seated garden seat or sofa – an ugly design and looked as if it would come to pieces if used.

School Childrens work.
The white sewing from school children was very poor – not representative & not up to the standard of what many of the schools can turn out – on the other hand there was some really good Knitting done by little girls.

Walking Sticks.
Not one walking-stick came! although many were asked for by intending buyers & could easily have been sold.

Lace.
Lace – there was not a great deal of this – & I think it did not sell very readily –

Thurs 26th Sep.
Travelled all night from Aviemore to Oban.

Friday 27th Sept.
Arrived at Oban at 4.30.a.m. went on board the steamer at 6. arrived at Castlebay, Isle of Barra in the evening after a very rough passage – felt more than half dead – stayed the night at the Inn. (Temperance One)

Sat 28th Sept.
Had a talk with my landlady Mrs. Jonathan MacLean who gave me the names of some really good knitters among the Fisher-girls, who are at present nearly all away at the English fishing (Yarmouth & Lowestoft) – but return to the Island at the end of November –

> The herring-fishing season was at it's height at this time. In the following year six hundred thousand tons of herring were caught, mainly by vessels out of Yarmouth and Lowestoft. In the Autumn, hundreds of Scottish 'fisher girls' could be seen gutting herring on the Denes.

I then called & saw Father Cameron and we talked about the Knitters.

Started at 12. mid day to drive to Eoligarry where I was to stay with the MacGillivrays – they had arranged various small meetings for me on the way round the Island – where I saw some of the best spinners & Knitters & weavers – especially at Skallery the home of Joseph MacLean, Merchant brother of Jonathan the Innkeeper – Mrs Joseph is very keen to help.
Around at Eoligarry in the evening.

Barra Crofter's wife riding to fetch 2 Creel loads of peats.

View in the Harbour of Castlebay Isle of Barra (the Land of the – MacNeils)

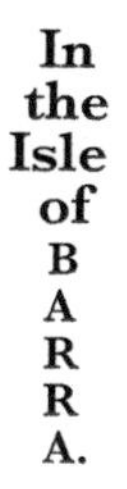

In the Isle of BARRA.

Loch Tangesdale & St. Clair's Castle.

Travelling – Stationery – & Postage Expenses from sun 15th to Sun 29th Sept 1912.

Category	Item	£	s.	d.
	Carried Forward.	8.	3.	7½.
Railway	Third return Railway Ticket – Oban to Perth.		16.	
	do do do do – Perth to St Andrews.		4.	6.
	Cabs St Andrews		2.	9.
	Porters, whole journey.		2.	6.
	Overweight luggage charged between St Andrews & Perth.		2.	
	Ticket for Typewriter, also charged at St Andrews –		1.	
Boat.	Steamers Oban to Barra.		15.	
Hiring.	Dogcart Castlebay to Skallery –		7.	
Stationery.	Writing paper –		1.	6.
	Envelopes		1.	
Telegrams.	Hon. Sec. (reply paid about the Tweeds for Canada)		1.	4½.
	Aviemore (postponing arrival – staying extra day St A.)			6.
	Ferguson, Lochboisdale. (about arrival there).			6.
Letters.	Miss Myra Warrand.			1.
	Hon. Sec. (3)			3.
	Hon. Treas.			1.
	Miss MacKintosh, Creagorry, Benbecula.			1.
	Postmaster Killearnan			1.
	Mr MacGillivray. Barra.			1.
	Mrs MacDonald. St Andrews.			1.
	Mrs. Stewart. Cupar Fife.			1.
	Miss Campbell, Kilberry (thanks for stockings)			1.
		11.	0.	8.

Eoligarry House Isle of Barra.

Built by an Old General MacNeil

100 years ago – but the top storey been burnt since then – it used to have a flat roof.

Sunday 29th September to Sunday 6th October 1912. (Eoligarry, Isle of Barra, Lochboisdale, South Uist.)

Sun. 29th. Sept.

Fine – The long drive to the United Free Church & back occupied most of the day – Settled to go all round the West side of the Island on Monday – and to the Isle of Eriskay on Tuesday – there are 500 inhabitants & a Priest in Eriskay – & the people are all engaged in fishing – so the girls are good knitters like in Barra.

Talked to the "Missioner" Mackay a little after church, about the Industries but his congregation very small – we were 13 all told.

Mon 30th. Sept.

Started off immediately after 8 o'clock breakfast, driving round the West side with Mr. MacGillivray – got within 3 miles of Castlebay (on Sat. when I arrived,we drove all round the East side) – so now have been all round this Island –

Visited several Townships & talked to a number of people, most of them prefer knitting to spinning which seems to be fast dying out – but I met two Weaveresses – gave one an order to make me some white (or rather cream) drugget –

One of the prettiest places we saw was Loch Tangesdale with St Clair's Castle in the middle of it on a small Island – most of the people busy with the Harvest – all Fisherman as well – and every Crofter wears sea-faring garb – It came on to blow tremendously & didn't promise well for Eriskay.

Out till past 8. having had nothing to eat all day except "a cup of tea in the hand" & a scone in one house about 4.30.! pretty well exhausted by the time we got in.

The Catholic Fishermen of Barra and Eriskay carried holy water in their boats and sprinkled their nets with it before fishing. Loch Tangesdale also known as Loch St. Clair is very well known amongst the angling community for it's excellent trout fishing.

Tues. 1st. October.

Storm and rain – impossible for the Fishing Smack to cross over to Eriskay – Wrote most of the morning & went out for a little later – but so windy & wet one could hardly stand –

John Macpherson, small merchant, came to see me – & brought me the names and present addresses (Yarmouth & Lowestoft) of several of the best knitters – I gave him one of the stockings sent by Miss Campbell, Kilberry – & he is to see that it gets passed round as a pattern –

The Campbell's of Kilberry Castle in Mid Argyle were landowners in a mainly gaelic speaking area, the family were interested in the antiquities and improving the culture of Scotland.

The other stocking Mrs MacGillivray is to take for me to a woman in the Tangesdale District – so that there will be one on each side of the Island –

Mrs Joseph MacLean would also be glad have one sent her.

Weds. 2nd. October.

Left Eoligarry about 10.a.m – drove the 10 miles in to Castlebay – bad road & very hilly so it took a long time – called to see John MacPherson at Northbay 9 the small merchant mentioned above) on the way and saw a half finished boy's Jersey made by a Widow MacKinnon – Beautiful knitting with a most intricate pattern on the shoulders – some of these patterns would be excellent for stocking tops –

Met a curious Funeral winding along over the sands & bent, to the burial ground, which is on a point of land on the West side – it was a poor young Fisherman who had died of consumption – leaving a wife, only married a few months – about 100 fisherman walking in couples led the way there then the coffin was carried in the middle of a group of women in their short striped drugget skirts with plaids and different tartans over their heads. – last of all a piper playing MacCrimmons lament – such a lovely morning & the beauty of the bright sun & yellow sands & blue green sea – somehow made it all the sadder –

At Castlebay, while waiting for the Steamer, I called on several people – & talked to Mrs Morrison of the Post Office & Mrs MacLean, Temperance Inn – & got more names of Knitters from them both – Went to see old "Mary" a weaveress – she was busy weaving white blanketing for fishermen's under garments – she is old & slow – can't do more than 2 yards a day – & is kept busy all the year round, so is not anxious for more work –

Went aboard the Steamer about 3. & reached Lochboisdale Pier about 6. after the usual pitching & tossing –

Drove 6 miles to Boisdale House on the south side of the loch – to stay with the Fergusons – he is a Merchant (here, at Lochboisdale Pier & in Eriskay) – Fish-Curer – & farmer combined & seems to be the great power in the South end of the Island – she is the daughter of the Rev. Nicholson U.F. Minister Dalibrog – 3 miles from here –

Thurs. 3rd. October.

Vey cold & showery – walked to some of the Crofts near at hand – not a great many workers – more spinning used to be done at one time – but there is no work for the Associations here now & the Merchants are not keen to buy Tweed as it's so difficult to get it sold again – found a few Knitters.

Friday 4th. October.

The Fergusons lent me a pony & I rode to Dalibrog in the morning – Called on the Rev. Nicholson & his wife and paid visits round there – & also in the Townships of Garrihillis – most of the people out in the Harvest field. – talked to a good many among the corn –

Sat. 5th. Oct.

– Rained without ceasing all day – did not go out – wrote letters etc.
Have settled to stay here till Tues. or Weds. going (or trying to go!) to Eriskay on Mon. or Tues. & then go to Milton Farm farther North in the Island – before crossing over to Dunvegan in Skye –

Two photograp[h]s. of Mrs MacDonald in North Uist (Cladach Kirkibost) dyeing wool – unconscious of the Kodak..

	Travelling & postage expenses from Sunday 29th. Sept. to Sunday 6th. Oct. 1912.	£	s.	d.
	Carried forward.	11.	0.	8.
Boat.	Steamer Barra to Lochboisdale, South Uist		2.	6.
	porters tips			6.
	Tip Eoligarry shepherd (who drove me to & from Castlebay – carried luggage up & down from the pier etc)		2.	6.
Telegram.	Mrs Macdonald. St Andrews – (asking for the lists of tweeds) –			6.
Letters.	Hon. Sec.			1.
	Mrs. Burnley-Campbell.			1.
	Mrs. Stewart, Cupar Fife			1.
	Mrs Macdonald, St Andrews.			1.
	Mrs Patten MacDougall, Gallanach (thanks for pair of pattern stockings) –			1.
	Messrs. MacDougall, Tailors, Inverness			1.
	Messrs Chalmers, do Oban.			1.
	Macdonald, Milton Farm.			1.
	Mrs Maclean, Carnan Inn. (about Drugget orders)			1.
	Miss MacKintosh, Creagorry (about yarn order)			1.
	Manager Dunvegan Inn.			1.
		11.	7.	7.

but she looked up immediately after and "posed" with her most Sunday expression & every muscle stiff & tense.

. . . .

This second photo is after she relaxed slightly & was just hearing " it is all over now"!

(she was very anxious to hide her bare feet – .

Sunday 6th. to Sunday 13th. Oct. 1912.
(Lochboisdale – Isle of Eriskay – Milton farm, S. Uist.)

Sunday 6th. Oct.

The Fergusons is a very strict United Free Household – drove to Daliburgh Church & sat through the Gaelic & English Services which came one on top of each other without breathing time – went into the Manse before & after Church so it was well past 4. o'clock by the time we got back for "dinner" – and it rained the last half of the drive.

Mon. 7th. Oct.

A stormy disagreeable sort of day – started in the morning riding Polly the red pony – posted letters in Daliburgh – & then visited people at the west side of the Township – a large one – most of them very slack whether they care to do any work or not – & some seemed to think it would be a special favour to me if they allowed their names to be put down as knitters or spinners – but I found one energetic family of MacLeods – they turned out to be the only Protestant family in the Township – the old mother spins & Lexie the youngest daughter knits really beautifully & can copy any pattern & "lift" it from a book too –

I made a long round home paying visits here & there– came across the "Machair", & tried a shorter cut still across the peat moss but it was too swampy for Polly so had to turn back –

Got home about 5 o'clock.

The ponies of the Outer Hebrides are generally small, round shouldered, and muscular, with thick and rough winter coats, while those of the Inner Hebrides are usually larger; Mull, Barra, Islay, Tiree, Skye, and Uist being the islands most noted for the good qualities of their ponies.

Tues. 8th. Oct.

Up early – Tremendous wind – but, hoping it might drop, started at 8. with Ferguson, my host, for the Isle of Eriskay – drove for about an hour to the extreme South of this Island – past Polichar Inn & all through what was once Kilbride Farm, but is now cut up into Crofts by the Congested Districts Board (known all over the Islands as the "C.D.B").– Very good crofts – as they are large enough & the people are doing well – the large ones are on the West side – the East is given up to Fishermen whose holdings are quite small but they have good new houses on them –

We left the dogcart at the nearest croft to the Old Farmhouse – or the ruins of it – it is where Flora MacDonald spent much of her young days and Prince Charlie slept there too I think – there is a huge old garden with a wall 20 feet high still intact – but the garden of course given up to sheep.

Flora MacDonald was the daughter of Ranald, son of Angus of Milton South Uist. She was born in 1722 and spent her early life in this part of South Uist.

From there on walked a couple of miles – hard work against the wind – then – waiting for Calmer weather, we visited several houses – all the women and girls good knitters and a few spin their own yarn –

As the wind showed no sign of abating – very high – dead against us but possible to sail across – and as I said I was prepared to try it – so set sail – the Mail Boat – manned by 3 men and a boy – Ferguson at the Helm – they made me sit in the bottom among the stones, for ballast – wrapped from head to foot in oilskins – the boat low in the water & so kept on shipping "seas" – so in a short time in spite of the oilskins, the water got down my neck & then penetrated all down the front of my coat by the fastenings – fairly cold & uncomfortable –

After 2 tacks when we were about in the middle of the Sound, the sail – a very old one – began to give way – and had to be hastily lowered & tinkered up – all the men bellowing suggestions to each other in Gaelic & hardly able to hear – it was very exciting to watch when the salt water wasn't getting into ones eyes! – & about that time I began to wonder whether we should ever reach the other side without capsizing. – after more tacks and beating about – we did – and went on landing to the nearest croft – had one of the inevitable "cups of tea" & tried to dry a little in front of the fire, but found the peat smoke on the top of the salt water rather trying to the eyes – and afterwards discovered that walking against the wind, which nearly lifted me off my feet, was the best way of drying!

The women thought me a sort of wonder of the world for coming across in such a storm –

The S.S. *Politician* sank in the Sound of Eriskay in 1941 and its cargo of whisky bottles was 'rescued' by the islanders. This true story was later turned into a book by Compton MacKenzie called 'Whisky Galore' and a film which was mainly shot on Barra. Today, Eriskay's only pub, Am Politician displays an account of the shipwreck.

Ferguson has a fish-curing "station" here, (Eriskay) – Cod & Ling – the work is mostly done by boys of 12 to 14. They have to spread out the fish to dry on the rocks – a man splits them – All the population living by the fishing – the men have boats– the boys work at the "station" & the girls go off to the gutting on the East Coast, via England – they are all away just now.

There is no road in the Island – just a good Pathway made by the 'Board' for the schoolchildren, who of course prefer to walk across country – however their parents like the path & it's convenient for Chapel. – the Catholic Chapel & Presbytery stand on one of the highest places in the Island & the school not far off –

We walked half round the Island, paying visits on the way – saw the place which sheltered Prince Charlie for 2 nights – and then walked – or rather struggled – wind tremendous – to his landing place – it's a raised green platform – fine natural turf – a wall was built round it afterwards by the people in memory of him – these walls are now flush with the ground, so one can sit on the grass and look straight out over the Atlantic – he was carried ashore on the Boatmen's shoulders & put down here – & out of his pockets he took handfuls of convolvulus seed from France which he scattered round him – they say there used to be one still growing but it's all been taken by Americans etc –

This beautiful beach is now called *Coilleag a'Phrionnsa*, which translates to "the Prince's cockleshell strand". It is home to the white striped pink sea bindweed, a flower not native to the Hebrides. The seeds are said to have fallen from Charles' pocket as he removed a handkerchief.

I lay down and rested on the grass & Gilhasbuig' MacIsaac, a fisherman who had come with us – sang – a lovely voice & a lovely Old Gaelic song –

We then climbed up to a Croft above – the house containing the father and Mother both with the old-age-pensions – 8 grown-up sons all fishermen – 3 daughters away at the English fishing – & one daughter in law sitting by the fire knitting.

They & Gilhasbuig & Ferguson, gave me the names of 40 or 50 good knitters – who will be returning to Eriskay in Dec and will like to knit all this winter.

After this we retraced our steps – personally I just had to lean back on the wind & get blown along & it was a relief.

We called at the Post office a wee thatched hoosie – & then at the Presbytery – & saw Father MacNeil (a native of Barra) – he says if I write to him any time about the Industries he will do all he can to help & will talk to the Fisher girls about it when they return – he showed me the chapel – built & decorated entirely by the Islanders themselves – & then walked down to the boat with us & saw us start.

The church was built in 1903 & is dedicated to St Michael the Archangel, one of the Western Isles' patron saints. His feast day is celebrated on 29 September each year and is traditionally marked by the baking of a special cake called the struan (*struathan*) It was baked on Michaelmas Eve by the woman of the house and was made in Barra as a layered bannock or cake. Great care and skill was needed in baking and an essential part of the ritual was the blessing said by the baker during the baking process. On the morning of the Feast Day all who were nearby go to an early Mass where the struan is blessed by the priest.

We pushed out a little way just to get alongside a new fishing-smack lying at anchor, which Ferguson wanted me to see – the "*Immaculata*", built at Banff cost £230. & she is the last cry in fishing-smacks – the crew of 6 welcomed us & we climbed on board & saw everything – they swung on down into the cabin (no companion way!) & I dropped onto a heap of fishing-nets – In the cabin they showed us the 6 bunks, 6 lockers & cooking-stove – then the table was pulled out & set up & we sat all round & listened while one of the crew "Archie" sang 3 or 4 Gaelic Songs – one he had sung to Mrs. Kennedy Fraser, & she had taken it down for her collection – these 6 men Ferguson says are the steadiest most trustworthy crew on the Island – he has lent them the money for the boat so ought to know.

We flew back before the wind to Kilbride – lovely it was – huge flights of wild geese accompanying us – their loud quacks rising above the roar of the sea & howl of the wind.

Landed about 6. walked the 2 miles to the cart & down back to Boisdale – pretty well tired out – but it was a most interesting & delightful day.

The boy on our boat was the great-grandson of the old woman who "saw"many things that have since come to pass – She lived at Kilbride & died about 20 years ago – Foretold all the deaths & marriages in South Uist during her day – the young men & girls used to go to her – & cross her hand with a bit of silver – & she would name the Bride or Bridegroom by description, never really by their name – & describe the place where they would meet – girls used to lodge with her during the fishing-season and she would terrify them by looking out at the door & "seeing" two great tall men 30 feet high with their arms stretched out side-ways – no girl dared venture over the threshold after dusk, – in that same place now stand the 2 huge cable-telegraph-posts exactly as she described them – only posts not men –

Then when she walked across the farm of Kilbride, she used to "see" cocks crowing and smoke rising from every knoll – just as it now is since the farm was cut up into crofts –

We saw the boys mother (granddaughter of the old see-er) in Eriskay – Ferguson asked her if she could "see" too – & she said "no, no, and indeed no" – but we both think she can as she has such strange eyes.

Ferguson said he too went to the old woman when he was a young man and not believing in her at all and she said "Yes" he would marry – & she saw him living in "a house on a big big hill – green to the top – with great white sheep without horns such as she nor anyone in Uist had ever seen at all – mixed with the black faced Highland sheep" Five years after that his father took the farm of Mingary(?) in Argyll for him & there he lived in this house on the big big hill green to the top & then ran Cheviot sheep among the black faced ewes – and there he married – (his wife is now dead – & he has married a new one).

In 17th Century in Scotland the most famous clairvoyant or predictor of the future was the Brahan Seer, known in the gaelic community as *Coinneach Odhar*.

Isle of Eriskay in the Outer Hebrides

This is where Prince Charlie first set foot in his own Country.

Weds. 9th. Oct.

Wrote letters and packed – leaving most of my things to go by boat to Boisdale Pier where I shall pick them up on Mon. 14th. Drove over to Milton farm in the late afternoon about 7 or 8 miles off.

Macdonald is the farmer who had to turn out of Vatersay after the Barra Raid about 3 years ago – he now has the 3 farms of Milton, Borinish & Ormiclat – a long stretch from sea to sea in the centre of South Uist – The household consists of his sister in law Mrs Boyd & his 3 daughters all grown up –

A nice old man whose wife's death years ago nearly broke his heart – & then came the trouble over the Barra Raiders & his only son turning out badly – so he is rather broken down altogether.

Since the late 18th century, Barra and many other islands had been overcrowded and by 1883 there were more landless 'cottars' in extreme poverty with no security of tenure than crofters and farmers. Having no other options people made 'land raids' onto other islands and set up new crofts which resulted in legal action being taken by landowners, court cases in Edinburgh and jail for the crofters. From Barra, families and cattle occupied the islands of Vatersay, Sandray and Mingulay, and a settlement with Lady Cathcart was not made until 1912, after many bitter disputes.

Mrs Boyd is a great knitter & would like to make money by it (she has a husband somewhere or other but seems to spend most of her time at Milton – I have bought a very good pair of stockings from her to use as pattern ones – & am getting her to knit another pair – if the yarn spun by Widow Fraser, Clachan , North Uist, which has just arrived & is very good indeed – the shop wool pair I will send to Eriskay to Father MacNeil.

Thurs. 10th. Oct.

Drove to the township of Stoneybridge with Katie the second daughter – a long drive – & visited 2 weaveresses & a spinner – & got the names from them of some others – very cold and wet.

The 2 oldest girls are both called Katie! & the youngest Mary – they all sing Gaelic songs & Mary plays Highland music so well – she is going to compete at the Mod next year –

They have told me of one or two good spinners about here – this farm is far away from most of the Townships but was the only available place to stay in & they are very kind about driving me to see the people –

Fri. 11th. Oct.

Drove with Katie the eldest one to the Townships of Howbeg – Howmore – Shishival – & Stillegarry & then onto Driomisdale Farm –

At Howbeg visited Widow Archie Lamont Mrs Ferguson, Clachan's sister she spins & was busy dyeing wool – then at Shishival saw the other sister Mrs George Lamont (they had married two brothers) she is also a great worker –

Then near Drimisdale went to the house of Widow Alexander Macdonald – she is the mother of Mrs. Ferguson, Clachan; & the spinner & dyer of the famous James Macdonald Plaid I have mentioned several times –

One of the finest old people I have met – 83. – tall – strong & full of life – no English of course – very clean – a real old darling – has given up weaving but spins always – up at 6 every morning & at her wheel by 7. – still makes suits for her family which is scattered, – the daughters all married in different parts of the Long Island & the sons in Australia, Africa & India – the last dead I think – she showed us a kilt she made for the soldier son over 30 years ago when he came home – She so hated his uniform that she set to work and made him a Macdonald Kilt & Doublet, carded – dyed – spun & wove it all herself – and today it looks like new.

Highland soldiers were recruited throughout the nineteenth century to serve in the British Army. They were famed for being taller and stronger than other Scottish recruits and were often leaving Islands where poverty was endemic.

She has promised to do the plaid for the order gained at St. Andrews – is to card – dye & spin it – and will help Mrs MacPhie, Gerinish to set it up in the Loom – & hopes to finish it before the winter. She lives in a beautiful spot on the shore of a loch near the ruin of a Clanranald Stronghold & looking up at Ben Mor & Heckla.

Another Mrs. Macdonald her near neighbour is also a good spinner & makes tweeds for the Fergusons at Druisdale Farm.

This Ferguson is uncle of Ferguson at Boisdale House & also of Mrs Maclean at Carnan Inn – We went up to Druisdale & had "tea" in the dining room with trout just out of the loch – that was about 7 o'clock. The Fergusons are such a nice family – he over 80 – she much younger & 2 daughters just grown up – they all take a great interest in Home Industries & will be very good to write to about the people in their district – they try to improve the mixing of the colours & the dyes –

By the time we left it was pitch dark & no lamps – we borrowed a stall lantern from the Fergusons – & this I had to hold down by the splashboard during the 9 miles home – a slow progress as it was a young horse who shied at most things, & in places the road is dangerous as there are several causeways across lochs & these are narrow with no sort of fences.

Sat. 12th. Oct.

Started early for the 15 mile drive to Carnan Inn – arrived somewhere about midday I imagine – but neither Eoghan the grieve who drove me nor I had a watch & there were no clocks at Carnan! –

Found Mrs MacLean waiting for me – with a good fire in the drawing room, where my cousin & I had spent 10 days just about a month ago – but the carpet had been changed for the winter one – a most affecting one of home-spun – Mill woven, rose colour & black sort of broken check –

Mrs MacLean handed me a letter from Mrs Farquhar MacMillan to myself – (she is a crofter's wife, the one whose house we waited five hours before going on board SS. *Hebrides*.) demanding to know what had become of the web of tweed 29 yards she gave me to send to St. A. & asking for it back by 'the next boat' if not sold! – I wrote a note explaining that as it had not been sold at St. A. it was being kept to take to the sale at Edinburgh in Dec. – but that if she really would rather get it back now she must write to Mrs Macdonald, Convener & ask for it –

I also asked Mrs MacLean to explain about it to her – poor woman, I hear they are badly in want of the money – & I hope it will be sold, but as far as I remember it was not a very attractive piece –

Mrs MacLean (post office as well as Inn) tells me that 4 or 5 letters with money have now come to the district from St. Andrews Sale which will be a relief to the people as some of them are growing anxious – it's very difficult for them to understand all the work that must be got through before the payments can be made –

I am going to send postcards to all among the people I know & whose tweeds were unsold – to tell them about Edinburgh – I am sorry I didn't think about putting a paragraph about it in the Oban Times with the account of the Sale –

Mrs MacPherson, Tailors wife Baledubh, Iochar, whose mother Widow MacAulay is going to spin part of the drugget ordered for St. Andrews – came to see me at the Inn – & I explained carefully, & wrote it down too, all about it – in 2 cases yarn to match is required as well – it took some time making all this understood.

Accomplished the drive home just before nightfall – the wind had risen to a hurricane & it was very cold & rain began just as we reached Milton – Eoghan & I who had talked Gaelic most of the way going subsided into silence except for an occasional "will Miss MacKenzie be dreadfully cold?" "Wild! Wild! but we will be getting back yet before the rain that is coming – and its we that should be thankful" –

Isabell, as a Gaelic Speaker, was able to understand all the subtle nuances of communication between people in the Islands, and her account gives a very rare insight into the culture she encountered on her travels.

Post-Office

Isle of Eriskay.

The telegraph pole is seen in the middle of the roof.

(The beautifully dressed youth near the door must be a Stranger from the South)

Travelling – Postage – Expenses from Sunday 6th. to Sunday 13th Oct. 1912.

		£	s.	d.
	Carried forward	11.	7.	7.
Hiring.	Box sent by Mailcart from Carnan Inn to Lochboisdale when I went to St Andrews (21 miles)		3.	6.
	Tip to stableman Boisdale (twice had pony to ride & had dogcart 3 or 4 times)		3.	
Telegrams.	Hon. Sec., about Winnipeg tweeds		2.	4.
	Payment for re-direction 4 wire from Hon. Sec.		1.	3½
	Porterage on 2 wires from Hon. Sec. (Daliburgh to Milton)			6.
Letters.	Mrs MacLean. Carnan Inn.			1.
	Mrs. Burnley-Campbell.			1.
	Mrs. Stewart, Cupar Fife.			1.
	Widow Fraser, Clachan, North Uist.			1.
	Typewriter Co. (order for writing-paper)			1.
Post-cards.	Killearnan, post-master			½
	Lochboisdale, do do			½
Sundries	Pair of stockings from Mrs Boyd, as a pattern pair.		5.	6.
	1 llb. yarn from Widow Fraser		2.	10.
	postage of the parcel of yarn			4.
		12.	6.*	11½
	(corrected March 1913. I.B.Mc.	~~12~~	~~7~~	~~9½~~

Flora Macdonald's Birthplace, South Uist

This picture of Flora Macdonald's Birthplace is a very bad one – it gives no idea of the real beauty of the spot And is taken, I think, looking South towards the Loch near Milton Farm.

List of Prize-Winners at St. Andrews Sale of Highland Home Industries 1912.

No. 1. Wood-Carving

1st. prize 25/-
2nd. prize 15/-
No Competition.

No. 2. Furniture

Class I.
1st. prize 30/- Not awarded
2nd. prize 15/- Colin Campbell. Kenmore. Inverary. (Arm-Chair).

Class II
1st. prize 15/-
2nd. prize 7/6.
No Competition.

No. 3. Metal-Work

Class I.
1st. prize 25/-
2nd. prize 15/-
No Competition.

Class II.
1st. prize 15/-
2nd. prize 7/6.

Wicker Work

No. 4.
Class I.
1st. prize 20/-
2nd. prize 10/-
3rd. prize 5/-
No Competition.

Class II.
1st. prize 10/-
2nd. prize 5/-
No Competition.

Class III.
1st. prize 5/- – Peter MacLeod, Baledubh, Iochar. South Uist. (Horse-collar).
2nd. prize Maggie MacKinnon, The Lane. Portree. Isle of Skye. (basket).
3rd. prize. Maggie MacKinnon – same girl – (Daffodil basket). *

No. 5. Walking-sticks

1st. prize 20/-
2nd. prize 10/-
No Competition.

No. 6. Plain White Sewing (school children)

1st. prize. 20/- Christina Macdonald. Glasphein, Glendale. Skye (chemise).
2nd. prize. 10/- Annie J. MacMillan. Dervaig Schoolhouse. Mull. Argyle. (white seam). *

No. 7. Lace.

1st. prize 20/- Christina MacLeod. Strathan. Lochinver. Lairg. (Irish crochet Blouse-set).
2nd. prize 10/- Nettie B. Campbell. Tarbert Lace School. (Handkerchief).
3rd. prize 5/-. Emma MacMillan. Tarbert Lace School.

No. 8. Stockings .

Class I. "Alloa"
1st. prize 5/-. Isabella MacLean. Gairloch. Ross-shire
2nd. prize 3/6. Alexina MacKenzie. do do
3rd. prize 2/- Annabella MacKenzie. do do
} 2nd. Prize Mrs A. Bain Gairloch *

Class II. Fingering
1st. prize 5/- K.M. MacKenzie. Torranahiliga. Gairloch.
2nd. prize 3/6.

No. 9. Best Web of Cloth.

1st. prize 40/- Mrs MacLean. Black Croft. Ledaig. (or MacLarren?) (woven by Mr Mowatt).
2nd. prize 20/- Mrs Angus Nicholson. Kallan. Isle of Grimsay North Uist.
3rd. prize 10/- Mrs Malcom MacRury. Stillegarry. South Uist.

No. 10. Highland Plaid .

1st. prize 40/- Miss Murray. Lairg. Sutherland.

2nd. prize 20/- Widow Hugh Murray. Blairich, Rogart. Sutherland.

No. 11. Floor Rugs.

1st. prize 20/- } No Competition.
2nd. prize 10/- }

No. 12. Carving in Celtic Design on Marble

1st. prize 20/- } No Competition.
2nd. prize 10/- }

No. 13. Homespun Yarn.

1st. prize. 10/- Widow Archie Ferguson. Knockintorran. North Uist.
2nd. prize. 5/- Christina Paterson. Borve. Isle of Berneray. North Uist.

Class I. consists of articles of the value of £1. & upwards.
Class II. do do do do do do do 10/- & under £1.
Class III do do do valued under 10/-

---

*. Competitors or names marked thus:– show an alteration between my notes & the printed list in '*Dro Greine*' – the names in brackets were from my notebook.

Sunday 13th. to Sunday 20th. Oct 1912.
(Milton, South Uist – Dunvegan, Isle of Skye).

Sun. 20th. Oct.
Rain, – Had a message in the morning, brought by the lassie, to say it was too wet for Church – & would I please have breakfast in bed – accepted it with pleasure! – and afterwards did a good deal of writing most comfortably – including diary for the week, which was rather long in consequence.

When I appeared at 2. o'clock dinner, the rest of the family was also making a first appearance – in fact, the Aunt, Mrs Boyd, & the "second" Katie never troubled to get up all day!

The Autumn of 1912 was a very cold and wet period in the Outer Isles.
The prolonged spell of depressed temperatures may have resulted from the eruption of a volcano (Katmai) in Alaska on 6th June, 1912.

However, thinking that a little fresh air & exercise would be good for this "elder" Cathie, Mary and myself – I made them come for a walk to show me Flora Macdonalds Birthplace – They led the way – about 2 miles along the road – then we crossed a bit of bog-land – & got into what seemed really a ruined township – the remains of so many buildings – It's part of what is now Milton Farm, but, that particular bit was once a good sized farm called Airidhmhullin – not being certain which of the ruins really was this birthplace – I took the precaution of walking inside the walls of each – a good many must have been byres etc – we finally found one rather larger than the others with a very slight attempt at a Cairn on one of the side walls (the walls are now only about 2 feet high) – we added three stones to it – & Cathie & Mary promised they will now go there often & always add a stone & will bring all their friends there too – I suggested that some of the really strong friends should be induced to lift into place a few of the big boulders which would give a firm foundation to the Cairn – We sat on the wall for about an hour & talked Jacobite days – it seems "Flora" was a relation of theirs – & their grandmother who lived to be over ninety, when she was a child talked to a "Herd" whose father was one of the boatmen who rowed the Prince over to Skye – or anyway rowed him somewhere – they were a little vague about this – but said they were so small when their Grannie was alive that they didn't remember much of what she used to tell them.

The Skye boat song lyrics were written by Sir Harold Boulton to an air collected by Miss Annie MacLeod (Lady Wilson) in the 1870s. Miss Macleod was on a trip to the Isle of Skye and was being rowed over Loch Coruisk, when the rowers started to sing the Gaelic rowing song, "*Cuchag nan Craobh*" (The Cuckoo in the Grove).

It was such a glorious evening – perfectly still after the rain & the hills quite clear except for a wee whisp of mist creeping up the foot of "Heckla' – Flora certainly first opened her eyes on a lovely view – the house was on a Knoll – facing East – straight onto Benmore & Heckla – with a few miles of Heathers & loch between, before reaching the foot of the hills – over that ground she must have walked carrying food for Prince Charlie when he was hiding in the cave at the foot of Benmore – on the other side, down by the sea – we wondered if she had to go right up & over the shoulder of the hill to get there – if so, it was a tremendous undertaking –.

Having looked East for a long time we turned round & by standing on top of the Cairn, could see the Atlantic – a goodish stretch of bog & machair & sand-hills in between us & it – on asking whether we could go home that way – they thought we might – so we went by a sheep-path winding in & out across the bog – the machair was easy walking as the harvest was all in (some of the crofters hadn't even cut theirs) –made a bee line for the sea – which we could hear thundering on the other side of the sandhills & then came out into a lovely little sandy bay – just opposite the setting sun – Rested on the bent for another half hour or so – And when we turned homewards to Milton – Benmore & Heckla had been almost black against the sky & their reflection in the waters of the loch was beautiful –

One felt thankful for the second perfect evening during two & a half months in this Long Island – the first was when I rode all along the shore of Loch Eport in North Uist – that was on the 12th. August – & now this.

Monday 14th. Oct.

Wrote some letters & talked "Knitting" with Mrs Boyd, who seemed very cheery after her quiet Sunday in bed –

Packed – Started after 2 o'clock dinner, for Lochboisdale to catch the steamer to Dunvegan, Isle of Skye.

Eoghan the Grieve, drove me the eight miles – the steamer (*Plover*) due at 4. so, as we were rather late, we had to hurry past the U.F. Manse at Dalibrog – I meant to have stopped to say goodbye to the Nicholsons.

At Lochboisdale had to wait a long time in the hotel – as it was the usual day of wind & rain – another world from the night before –

To my joy unearthed the travelling Bath which had left London at the beginning of August – & never been heard of since! – it turned out to have been sitting for over a month, in the store on the Pier – the Agent – who is also Postmaster & had known all my addresses for quite a month – said he didn't know where I was! & so he couldn't let me know about it – As it seemed a useless waste of breath to expostulate, I just had to smile – & pay a bill of 1/- for something – probably for his trouble in housing the bath.

When SS. *Plover* came in, heard we should be very late getting to Dunvegan owing to the stormy weather – so took a cabin – & had a vile crossing – making Dunvegan at 3 in the morning – feeling very sorry for myself indeed!

Tuesday 15th. Oct.
"Mr. Budge" of the Hotel was waiting there – & having secured a suit-case & a holdall & not caring a scrap what happened to anything else, we stumbled side by side along the pier in pitch darkness to where the Hotel motor was – got into it with 3 "Anglers" from Lochmaddy & a mountain of fishing rods and landing nets – & was whirled half a mile or so to the Hotel – where I retired to bed for the whole day! did a few letters in the afternoon.

Weds. 16th. Oct.
Incessant wind & rain – couldn't go out – & anyway still felt rather exhausted from the Minch – wrote a good many letters.

Thurs. 17th. Oct.
Rain morning – Cleared up later. Went to tea at Dunvegan Cottage with the MacLeods –

'MacLeod' told me a good deal about St Kilda & the tweeds – besides owning the Island he supplies them with meal, flour & groceries too sometimes! – & they pay their rent & pay for their supplies in tweed and feathers – but, as there has been no demand for tweed this year he has hundreds of yards of it lying in his storehouse –

All the crofters owe him money! Their reported 'starving' condition this year was, of course, un-true, they were short of tea, & tobacco & other luxuries, but the necessities of life, such as meal & flour, they had plenty of.

Mrs Anstruther Gray (wife of the member for St. Andrews) was at tea there too – it was interesting meeting her as they have Langadh Lodge & shooting in North Uist & no word to see them motoring past Clachan pretty often! – We walked back together to the hotel where they are staying the night & talked a good deal about Uist & the tweeds – She said they hear a good many grumbles from the workers about being paid " in kind" by the Scottish Home Industries – but I told her if they like , they can take the money instead – the smallness of the profit she also deplored – she likes the people so much, they will be there next year agin I think. The show at Cladach Kirkibost (the one I wanted to go to after we left Westford Inn but could not manage to get back again across the North Ford) she says was very good indeed – some excellent tweeds and knitting.

Fri.18th Oct.
Spent most of the day writing – in the evening went to see Mrs MacLean, the Bakers wife who is rather an authority on home-dyes – (she was governess to Mrs Stewart's children –

Cupar Fife – the one who is selling the Homespun yarn so kindly) she told me of one or two good knitters in this neighbourhood – but said (what others have also said) that there is little or no spinning – & no weaving – all the wool is sent to the Patons Mill – there is one girl who knits golf jerseys – sold round at the small 'Show' here in Aug.

One dye she mentioned which I had never heard of, but, I daresay is well known? it is that common grass makes a lovely green with a little coppereas added – also for another green there is the plant she called "*guiseach*" & described as the flower like a thistle which has no prickles I don't know it's name – All of the other dyes she talked of were ones one already knew. I asked her to try & find out what they use for 'Red' & she is to consult some very old woman she knows & will write & tell me –

Mrs MacLean herself does no spinning, but used to help her mother with the dyes when she was small.

Cuiseag. A species of grass,having a slim straight stem , *Cuiseagach* – full of slender stalks and stems. Definition from an older out of print Gaelic dictionary.

Miss MacLeod came to see me in the evening to tell me not to go by mail cart after all to Husabost to see her sister Mrs Martin – as she had not gone there herself (we had arranged she was to tell her sister to expect me at breakfast time!)

At my evening meal had the society of Mr Wilson, Lochmaddy, (Congested Districts) & his clerk – Since I first saw him at Carnan Inn Iochar I'd heard from about a dozen people that he is the greatest scoundrel un-hung – in the whole of the Long Island! never 'true' to what ever side he is working for – He is very plausible & interesting to talk to & full of enthusiasm for the good of the Islanders – did a good deal of agitating at the time of the "Barra Raid", in those days he happened to be Lord Dunmore's factor in Harris!

He told me they would be very pleased to see me in `Kilmuir – "they" the Land Commission or whatever they are called – are going to spend the winter in Skye.

In 1844 the Earl of Dunmore directed some of the weavers in Harris to copy the Murray tartan in 'tweed', and the result was so successful that he adopted it for his keepers, ghillies, and other retainers, besides using it for his own wear. It was seen that a material could be produced for which an outside sale might be hoped, and Lady Dunmore devoted much time and thought to the introducing of the tweed to her friends, and then to the improving of the process of production.

Sat. 19th. Oct.

Rain – made enquiries about Husabost – 9 miles off – thought of walking there & getting the hotel motor to fetch me – ended instead by taking a ' machine' to go there & back as it was so hot – Started after lunch, having wired to the Martins to expect me – Mr Martin is a Gaelic speaker – he & Mrs Martin told me a good deal about the Industries –

or the absence of Industries! but, they said it's most difficult for the Local show comm to get together any tweeds at all – that this year they had 3 prizes only – & that sometimes a woman will say " I will be sending some just to please you" – it's a pity but it shows I suppose that they can't be really in want of money – & as there is already more tweed on the market than can be disposed of it does not really much matter –

They say some very good Shetland Shawls are knitted, also stockings, & a certain amount of yarn spun.

Mrs Martin in talking of basket-making said that some very good willows are grown in Dunvegan by Mr John Mackenzie, MacLeod's Factor – & that someone had once started basket-making there – that it languished for 2 years & then died out altogether –

On my way home I stopped at Dunvegan School & saw Graham the schoolmaster – he & his sisters gave me the names of a weaver & a few spinners near Uig which is their home –

I went to MacLeod telling him all about the Canadian scheme for tweeds – thinking he might possibly care to send some from St Kilda out there.

I also went to see the Miss Mackenzies the Factors sisters who manage the local Show & they are going to let us have the names of all the Exhibitors & workers.

"MacLeod" & his Factor John MacKenzie

among the Herring- Barrels at Dunvegan Pier.

Fish Curing "Station" Dunvegan Pier

A "Crew" of Barra Girls working (the girls heads show just above the barrels but are difficult to make out.).

Travelling & Postage Expenses from. 13th. to 20th. Oct. 1912.

Category	Item	£	s	d
	Carried forward	12	6	11½
Travelling	Tip to Grieve, Milton, S. Uist.		5	0.
	Steamer Lochboisdale to Dunvegan		7.	6.
	Porters		1	0.
Stationery	Ream Writing paper & postage of parcel		4	6.
Hiring	Dogcart Dunvegan to Husabost		12	6.
	Carried forward	13.	17	5½
Telegrams	U.F. Manse, Kilmuir (form enclosed askin them to wire).			6.
	Mis Martin Husabost			8.
	Dunvegan Hotel (from Lochboisdale, about meeting me)			6.
Letters	Orders for knitted goods for Miss Myra Warrend for Canada.			
	Mrs. Robertson. Newton Farm. N. Uist.			1
	Mrs Angus John Ferguson. Knockintorran. N. Uist.			1
	Marion MacCorquodale. Cladach Kirkibost. N. Uist.			1
	Mrs MacDonald. Post Office. Isle of Berneray N. Uist			1.
	Mrs Gillies, U.F. Manse. Clachan. N. Uist			1.
	John MacPherson, Northbay. Isle of Barra.			1.
	Miss Myra Warrand (2)			2.
	Hon. Sec. (3)			3.
	Mr MacGillivray, Eoligarry, Isle of Barra.			1.
	Mrs Burnley Campbell (2)			2.
	William MacKay Esq. Inverness			1.
	Mrs MacDonald. St Andrews (2)			2
	Ferguson, Lochboisdale			1.
	Cathie Macdonald, Milton (also, knitted order for M.W.).			1
	Mrs Macdonald, U.F. Manse. Kilmuir. Skye			1.
	Rev. MacPhail. Ch. of Scotland Manse do do			1.
	Postmaster, Portree.			1.
	Mr Fraser, Solicitor, Portree (Basket Making)			1.
	MacKay. Merchant. Portree			1.
	MacNab. Schoolmaster. Kilmuir			1.
	MacDonald. Schoolmaster. Uig.			1.
	Lady Marjorie MacKenzie (about Gairloch)			1
	Mrs Patten MacDougall			1
	Editor *An Dro Greine* (2) forgotten from 2 or 3 weeks ago			2
	do *Oban Times* (3)			3.
		14.	1.	11½

Sunday 20th. to Sunday 27th. October 1912. Dunvegan – Kilmuir (Kilmaluug, Staffin) Skye).

Sun. 20th Oct.

Wet, wrote diary. Had tea with the MacLeods of MacLeod at Dunvegan Cottage – Talked of St. Kilda Tweeds & Canada – MacLeod thinks of sending out some of it on the same terms as Miss Myra Warrand is doing with the Council.

Mon. 21st. Oct.

Went to the Factors' office (Mr. John MacKenzie) in the morning & met MacLeod there – & we went down to the Storehouse on the Pier to see the 2000 yards of Tweed – Beautiful Tweed – Arranged that 12 webs of them from 30 to 33 yards each should go to Canada & wired to Miss Myra Warrand asking if she would take it on exactly the same terms as the tweed she is taking from the Council.

Returned to lunch at the Cottage – first seeing all over the Castle which is full of interest – Got the answer to the wire in the evening agreeing to take the tweed.

View of Loch Snizort from the road

Tues. 22nd. Oct.

Left Dunvegan in the morning – Motored the 35 miles to stay with Rev & Mrs Macdonald at the U.F. Manse, Kilmuir – Delayed by punctured tyre near Edinbane. Stopped at Snizort Post Office to talk to Flora MacKintosh, whom I used to know & find she still goes in for spinning yarn –

Reached Kilmuir about 3. o'clock. After tea the Rev. Macdonald walked with me to the Skye Osier Co. Factory – where we saw Keighley the manager for a few moments & he said he would show me everything next morning.

Called also at the Schoolhouse & saw MacNab, Headmaster & the 2 assistants Miss Macdonald & Miss MacLean – Then on to the Post Office to see Mrs Gillies, who is a good spinner & her daughter a good knitter.

when the tyre punctured.

Wed 23rd Oct.

Lovely morning – Walked down to the Basket Factory – it is called (The House of the Willows) – Its a long wooden shed with large windows & doors the centre stacked with willows ready for use & with finished Herring-baskets. – the lads work all along the sides with their backs to the walls sitting at it rather like Tailors only with their legs stretched out straight in front of them – at the end of the building in an inner room where are stored all kinds of wicker furniture chairs – tables – clothes. baskets – lunch-baskets, work-baskets etc etc. Splendid things very strong & well made. (I spied one settee like the one I saw at St Andrews – & it was the only thing of the whole lot that didn't look strong & was also of an ugly design, not even comfortable to sit in – it seemed a pity they had not sent some of their other things as I am sure they would have sold well & also would have won prizes) – At present they make these things "to order" only – as they are working hard at the Herring-baskets – Keighley is very pleased about these baskets & he has invented a way of strengthening the handles & bottoms by inserting strong wire & he says they are found to be very good – he is very keen – & told me a great deal about everything – the following are the rough figures he gave me – but as he is the practical working manager on the spot & does not really have much to do with figures, so the statistics are most likely very 'rough' as he spoke without referring to any notes to guide him: –

The Factory was started by Dr. Barbour 3 years ago last March – there are now 13 lads working – when they begin to learn the trade they start at 3/- a week & can get as much as 8/- while still learners – Later, when they can make the things quite alone,

– they may earn as much as 20/- a week – it is the "piecework" – They are all lads who <u>have</u> to live at home on the crofts for various reasons & of course often go off work for a day or two at a time to attend to the crofts at home –

They are now working at a 'large' order for their "Quarter-Cran Herring-Baskets" – have to turn out 100 gross by the end of June, trying to make 2 gross a week, but cannot quite manage this –

The Cran has been a term in use in the fishing industry from the 18th century. Mainly used as a unit of measure to describe, landed uncleaned herring from the North Sea. In 1852 it was defined as the equivalent of one standard box of about 37.5 imperial gallons, the average catch being about 750 fish.

baskets sell at 25/6 per doz (when taken by the gross).
do do do 27/- do do (when sold in single dozens).

making per doz costs 20/-
freight do do do 3/- to 4/-
payment of "Traveller" do do do 1/-

Thus having a margin for profit of 6d. to 1/6
per doz.

This year about 43,000 Herring Baskets have been sold in Scotland – of these: –

15,000 are made in Aberdeen
14,000 " " " Edinburgh & Leith
6,000 " " " Skye Osier Co. (which comes 7th. on the list)

More profit could be made if the Willows were all grown at home – as it is many of them come from Holland & Germany.

Cost of Willows per Ton.

Foreign	from	£11.10.0. to	£15.10. 0.
do Freight of		3. 0.0.	3. 0. 0.
		£14.10.0	£18.10. 0.

Home Grown. £12. 0. 0. to £14. 0. 0.

Keighley then took me down to the Companys' Croft to see the willows they are growing there – Five acres framed in on a sloping piece of ground – of this about an acre and a half is planted – there are patches of third years, second years, & this years growth.

I rather think this plantation is intended more as a lesson to Crofters on how to grow them, than as a supply for the 'Company', although it answers both purposes of course – Keighley says they are very good willows – the firm kind are the most valuable.

Some of the crofters in this district have planted patches of them, with varying results. – The Congested Districts Board supplied the plants in most cases I think – the first year there is a great deal of work in keeping the ground clean – then fences are a difficulty as cows get in & eat up the willows! Then the whole process of preparing them ready for use is such a new one – & the average Skyeman does not take quickly to new ways & ideas –

When the willows are cut, in Spring, just before the sap rises, they are placed in the ground (or in water I forget which he said!) – till they show signs of sprouting – then the bark is stripped off & they are stacked to dry in the wind which is better than the sun as it has the effect of discolouring them.

And, although it is a paying crop, 4 tons per acre in a good year – not a great many have gone in for it –

One great advantage of this wicker-work factory is, that in it these lads learn a real trade – not just a means of making a little extra pocket money – which should be useful to them in whatever part of the world they may eventually find themselves.

Keighley thinks the Company would 'pay' once the lads have made a start & now the Herring Baskets are so successful – if they could reduce the freight bill (about £73. on importing foreign willows last year) & if they had a real market for their goods –
His wish is to see a Central depot in Glasgow – with their own "Traveller" (or the share of one with the tweeds etc) –

It's just the same as the other Home Industries – no real market –
In the afternoon went to the school – there are 100 children, but quite 20 were away at the Harvest – MacNab, the headmaster, told them about the Industries and called for a show of hands of those whose mothers spin & knit – more than half their hands flew up in the air– for both– but not for tweed making –

Two little boys wearing tweeds made by their mothers were next pounced upon & dragged forth by Miss Macdonald 2nd Teacher, for my inspection! much to their embarassment & mine too, as I felt so for them, guessing how they would be teased about it afterwards! especially as their poor little breeks were very much patched and worn, but the situation was redeemed by all the boys whose stockings were home knitted having to hold out a leg to show them off – & this meant all the boys in the school! –

School dismissed – the two under-teachers Miss Macdonald & Miss MacLean said they would take me to see some of the mothers – So we walked off & did a good long round –

In a Shepherd's house I saw the best yarn I have seen yet – finer & softer than the first prize at St Andrews – quite as good as the Gairloch yarn, which is the best I know, so far, – This yarn (Mrs Beeton's) won first prize at the Congested Districts Board Agricultural Show in Kilmuir this year – it's a twist of 3 colours – marvellously firm and soft – but Mrs Beaton has very little time for doing it – owing to a very large family, but her two eldest girls (Cathie & Katie as usual) are good knitters of Shetland Shawls – Their Shawls seem very popular in Skye – the girls like working them better than socks & stockings – they are quicker to do & make more show!

By 1912 a specialist firm in Nottingham was producing gossamer fine knitted shawls in the 'Shetland' style. Up until the closure of the Highland Home Industries shop in Edinburgh in the 1970s, handmade knitted shawls from Shetland and the Islands could still be bought. This luxury, specialist niche market continues today.

Mrs Gillies of the post-office was another we went to see – (my second visit to her). She showed us blankets & yarn of her own spinning – the yarn, a twist of 2 colours, very firm indeed but just a little hard.

The 2 teachers say they would like to undertake to look after & get carried out, all orders for knitted goods or tweed or yarn – The Council may send to the District of Kilmuir & will do all the writing in connection with it – I said I thought the Council will, besides paying postage of letters, devise a scale for some small payment of say any order that may go through their hands – such as 1^{d}. per pair socks, 1½^{d} stockings, 1½ per 2 ½ cuts of yarn. Perhaps 1^{d}. per yard of tweed (but there will anyway be so very little of this – it hardly counts) 2^{d}. or 3$^{d.}$ for a large shawl or Golf jersey –

Settled to go & see more people with Miss Macdonald on Saturday afternoon. Both of these Teachers are particularly nice & very anxious to do all they can – Miss MacDonald lives at home with her mother who has a croft near the school & Miss MacLean comes, I think from Uig (5 miles off) – They both seem certain that a great deal of good knitting might be done in Kilmuir during the winter months – & that the people would be only too glad to earn some money in this way – the Macdonalds at the Manse say the same – they are very lucky in having had a Miss Russel, U.F. Church Mission lady worker for 4 years (she has now left & gone to Isle Ornsay) who used to hold classes where the girls worked at sewing & knitting for Foreign Missions & had Bible Readings afterwards – anyway during that time she taught them to make all sorts of things & no end of new stitches & patterns – at the other end of the Parish in Staffin there is one of their mission lady's [*sic*] a Miss Kirk whom I hope to see – they say she would organize knittting in that part of the district – There is so much wool to be had as most of these crofters have a good many sheep –

> The United Free Church of Scotland had missionaries whose aim was to evangelise in rural areas. There were many revival organisations involved in Missionary work in the early twentieth Century, in the Outer Isles. e.g the Faith Mission had links to a Bible College in Edinburgh.

One very strange thing which I can't understand is, that in Kilmuir the <u>highest</u> price paid for wool (black faced) is 14/- per stone – often only 12/- – while in the Uists only the other side of the Minch the lowest price for the same kind of wool is 18/- per stone – & sometimes 20/-

Thursday 24th Oct.

Wrote letters all the morning – In the afternoon visited several houses with the Rev. Macdonald – "Monkstadt" among others – one of the haunts of Prince Charlie & Flora Macdonald – It is now belonging to the C.D. Board & is used as a stud farm with a manager living in the old barn.

Here also some splendid willows are grown –

Got back to the Manse in time to attend the part for the "Church Mission Work Class" – about 8 young women – this was a friendly party to meet me – not to work – We all sat round in a circle in the drawing room – & as no one else would utter I had to make heroic efforts to overcome my own shyness & talk hard – but it's very trying having 16 eyes glued on to every idiotic word one says! – the party went on for hours & hours, one lady perched on the music stool must have grown very tired – All 'business" talk was to be reserved till after tea – so conversation was rather limited but they were all very nice. Tea was a serious business, one had to eat & eat, not only did I find the 2 ladys on either side of me passing scones & jam on me, but the two opposite as well – till I began to dread that the glaring lamp seated in the middle of the table would also politely stoop & hand me the butter!

Afterwards tongues wagged more freely in the drawing room – with the result that Miss Macdonald (my hostess) agreed to form a Committee of all those present including the 2 school Teachers – some, very few, will do knitting themselves, but they mostly said they had "no time", one, called Johan, especially was very haughty – her high forehead & beautifully polished temples with each hair strained back to bursting point & a very tight mouth – struck awe to one's heart the moment one met her – She it was who later had to be "pressed" for half an hour before she would sing – She finally graciously consented, & with marvellous aplomb "lifted" a hymn in a piercing voice – just from where she sat in the circle with no accompaniment at all (Nurse Ross, offered to play for her but she paid no heed to her) – &, having once begun, she favoured us with 4 or 5 one after the other – I kept my eyes fixed on the hearthrug in grim determination not to let the corners of my mouth get out of control!

The party ended about 11 o'clock with prayers.

At the same time as Catholic Missionaries were travelling up the Hebrides from Barra, the Protestant Society for the Propagation of Christian Knowledge (SPCK) was spreading the Gospel south from Lewis. Although the majority of the population of Barra and South Uist practised a pre-reformation style of Catholicism from the time of St.Columba, Protestant enclaves were established by 1912.

Friday. 25th. Oct.

Up early and started off for a long round with the Minister (34 miles altogether) a perfect day – clear – frosty & sun shining – "Tommy" the horse, just "off grass" had to be urged with the butt end of the whip & a continued chant of "come up Tommy, come up Tommy, there's a good laddie – trot! now! trot! that's it"

We went round by the ruins of Duntulm Castle – Kilmaluag – Digg (?) – Staffin – & onto the end of the road – in fact on down round the North end of Skye from West to East – from a magnificent view of Harris & the Lewis to an equally lovely one of "Scotland"–

Everywhere the harvest was in full swing. The 'end of the road' will soon no longer be the end – as a new bit is being made by the Board to join it from Portree – this will bring the people of Staffin within 10 miles of the 'metropolis' instead of 30 as they now are –

The harvest scene which was common in remote parts of rural Scotland, was of haystacks and corn stooks with bare patches of unharvested potatoes, typical of the rural peasant subsistence agriculture of the late 19th century.

We stopped & called at three schools – Kilmaluug – Digg (?) & a new one in Staffin (not the big one farther on) – the minister extracted various writings in the books – & heard the Gaelic Bible Reading – & I talked a little about Industries – Then we called on Miss Kirk – (the lady worker) but unfortunately she was away in a distant township –

About 4 o'clock we came to old Donald Ross the Church Elder's house – here Tommy was un-harnessed & we were given 'tea', (by that time we were rather in want of a little something to keep off the pangs of starvation – it's so awkward these long expeditions as a guest – as one can't fill one's pockets with biscuits & chocolate – one day in the Outer Isles I did have some chocolate with me – but never got a chance of eating it – & this modern version of " Tantalus" was the last straw – so now I never take any with me) –

Donald is blind in both eyes – 83 – & an old darling – the little new stone U.F. Church is the pride of his life (he gave over £100. towards building it) – after tea I Kodaked him & the minister standing against the vestry door – Donald in his "black" coat & sort of top hat –

U.F. Church Staffin
and
Donald Ross "Elder".

On the way home, we again tried to see Miss Kirk – but she had not returned –

Went back by Quiraing – most beautiful although it was growing too dark to see very well – we both got out & walked up the pass – Tommy going on ahead on the extreme outside edge of the road – The Minister has to do this drive every 3 or 4 Sundays as he has 2 little churches to preach in –

The last 8 or 9 miles it rained & was very dark (no lamps as we had been looking forward to the moon!) – arrived about 10 o'clock & had another tea with cold sardines! –

Saturday 26th. Oct.

Wrote letters in the morning – started walking with my hostess about 2. o'clock to meet Annie Macdonald, Teacher – at the Post-office –

We went first of all to see the one weaver in the district Donald Nicholson, (Hungladder, Kilmuir.) (Mrs Macdonald came because she had never seen a loom being worked! she is a native of Shetland) – Donald & his sister Mary live in a wee "Black house" – very tidy & as clean as it's possible under the circumstances – the loom – a small old one – fills half the house & the peat reek the other half – He is a very good weaver but doesn't get enough work , so he also acts as 'navvy' breaking stones & mending the roads –

> The Congested Districts Board could buy land and improve it , by building roads and draining ditches. The stones for hard core were usually broken by hand, by navvies or nappers, as they were called in Lowland Scotland.

Most of the people send their wool to the Paton Mills. He says he can weave any Clan Tartan & some years ago made Macdonald Tartan stair carpets for Duntulm House – He weaves rather slowly – about 6 yards a day – but it is good work – his sister Mary spins a good deal –

That visit over, Mrs Macdonald left us – & we went onto a tiny "shoppie" Kept by Mary Macdonald (sister of Mrs Gillies of the Post office), a dear old person with light blue eyes – she used to spin a great deal but now only does enough for her own use – she showed us some wonderful petticoats of tartan drugget (not clan tartan), some of the very, very firm kind that looks like cotton altogether but is really wool as well –

> The most common drugget skirt, was of coloured stripes, often referred to as 'strippet petticoats' in Scottish Folk songs. Drugget had a linen warp and a wool weft and it was striped in the direction of the warp in different colours. Much later drugget made from a cotton warp became available. It was a fabric that people would buy in the mainland and rarely was it made on a loom at home. Today in Kihnu, a world heritage site in the Baltic Sea, the same drugget skirts are worn everyday by the women on the Island. Men did not wear drugget.

Next to a MacKenzie Croft – all the family employed in the stack-yard – Bella – one of the daughters would like to do knitting this winter – but is also on the lookout for a place as childrens under-nurse – (she is 20, & was trained as a school teacher, but failed in the final exam).

Here we are joined by Nurse Ross, such a very nice woman, one of the Queen's Nurses – comes from Inverness – she is to be one of the work committee – the people are devoted to her & she to them – We turned Eastwards up the hill through the old Burial ground & looked at Flora Macdonald's tombstone – a high Celtic Cross – it can be seen for miles around – a gaunt white ghost showing against the hillside –

From there did a whole number of visits – such delightful people – & saw some very good knitting – shawls – petticoats – motor scarves – golf jerseys – socks etc.

In another MacKenzie house had another 'cup tea in the hand' – Before this is a house where the mother is very ill with consumption, Nurse Ross left us – We went to 3 "Black" houses – although there are not a great many left in Kilmuir now-a-days – inside the mother was half paralyzed & looked in pain & hopeless sitting in the middle of the room over the peats – her daughter is a very good knitter – she had the same hopeless look in her eyes as the mother –

The Blackhouse was a small, traditional stone-built house, common in the Highlands and Islands. The outer walls were generally built as a double dry stone wall, wooden rafters, dry packed earth floor and thatched roof made of turf with straw. There was no chimney, the peat fire being in the middle of the house and the smoke permeated the roof covering, which was used as fertiliser when it was removed in good weather. The house was home to both people and livestock.

The wind had risen – straight against us & rather a struggle to get home in the dark 'cross country about three miles – then the moon appeared & it was easier – around about 8.30 late for "tea" & very tired.

	Travelling & Postage Expenses 20th. to 27th. Oct. 1912.			
	Carried forward	14	1	11½
Hiring	Motor Dunvegan to Kilmuir (35 miles).	1	10	
Telegrams.	Prepaid Miss Myra Warrand about St Kilda Tweeds		1	8½
	United Free Manse, Kilmuir			6.
	Postmaster Portree			6.
	Miss Myra Warrand		1	0.½
Letters	Sending letter by a Messenger to 'MacLeod'			6.
	Mrs Burnley Campbell			1.
	Miss Myra Warrand (2)			2.
	Mrs Angus Macdonald, Balemore. N.Uist (yarn order)			1.
	Factor,Dunvegan (St Kilda Tweeds)			1.
Post-Cards.	Post-master Portree			½
	Post-master Killearnan			½
		15	16	8½

Sunday 27th October to Sunday 3rd Novembr 1912.
(Kilmuir, Skye ....Portree, Skye)

Sunday. 27th. Oct.
Wet – Wrote diary, Very tired from the last 2 days – Didn't go out at all.

Monday 28th. Oct.
Wrote nearly all day – Packed – left the Manse Kilmuir, about 8 in the evening – drove the 5 miles into Uig with Rev Macdonald who was going to a "conference" at Inverness – then got into the Motor-Mail-Coach – arrived Scorrybruck, Portree about 11.30 – the coach having deposited my luggage and me on the roadside a quarter of a mile from Scorrybruck – the driver waved his hand into the dark in the direction of the house – & off he drove – found my way with some difficulty down a steep hill & through the farmyard in the dark – & a boy went up & brought the luggage down one by one. –

My new landlady (from Glasgow) had forgotten to light the fire which I had ordered in my room!

Tuesday 29th Oct.
Wet – Answered a whole budget of letters. Lunched with Lady Macdonald – at Portree Lodge.

Went afterwards to the Tweed Mills with Miss Macdonald. It seemed so odd to see the whole process being done with lightning speed by machines after the hundreds of hand workers one had watched in the last three months – They have some very pretty colouring among their tweeds. Also some beautifully soft imitation Shetland material – all double width (about 7/- a yard).

This Mill sends all it's finished stuff to the Inverness Mills where it is sold – so – none of it is sold locally.

Wednesday 30th October.
Rain – Lunched at the Lodge – having written letters most of the morning. Afterwards Miss Macdonald took me to see Miss Cameron, the Basket-work Teacher – A little hunch back – so nice & so intelligent & everyone says is one of the few energetic people in Portree!

She showed us whole stacks of baskets ready for sale. – just now there are only 8 girls in her class – as – not being a permanent trade some of them go off every year – to service – or something – but those who are working at it can add considerably to their income (!) by it & are very fond of the work –

In other places in Skye, I have heard this industry referred to as the "Portree Toys" – but – as far as they go – they are quite good work – neatly finished off – not strong – but the material (sort of split cane) is not strong – they sell well at Bazaars & are also bought a great deal locally by Tourists – The Workshop also has a window which displays a few specimens for sale – we were at her house, but she promised to let me go to the workshops another day & see some of the girls making the baskets.

With the 'By-Name' running in my head, I asked if she ever thought of making dolls tables – chairs – basinettes etc – & she rather liked the idea – will try some herself –

Settled to go to the workshops on Fri.after.

Thursday 31st. Oct.

More rain. Wrote all the morning – In the afternoon had an appointment with Mr.Fraser, Solicitor who 'runs' the Basket-Making Industry – had a long talk with him & he gave me the Abstract of their accounts, as to the number of baskets made & the number of girls working, for the last few years from 1908 in fact. Also let me see a 'Report" he had written on the Industry for Dr. Scott (Lecturer on Political Economy for the University of St Andrews) who is inquiring into Scottish Home Industries in the areas under the Congested Districts Board –.

Mr. Fraser seems to have tried his very hardest to make the baskets a successful Industry – hunted about till he found the cheapest place to buy the materials from – written to numbers of large shops etc to try & get a sale for them – usually met by the answer that foreign things are cheaper! – Had found out all about the working of Willows too – wanting (which also struck me) to make more serviceable baskets – want of funds – the smallness of their workshops – & no market – all stand in the way –

In fact it's very existence seems to depend on the energy of these 2 people – Mr. Fraser & little Miss Cameron – As well as the kindness of Mrs MacKinnon – She & her friends have been the chief buyers all the time.

		1908.	1909.	1910.	1911.
Baskets & Trays.	Number in hand beginning of year		82.	121.	141.
	do made during the year.	538.	546.	746.	854.
	do sold do do do	456.	507.	692.	795
	do in stock at end of year	82.	121.	141.	200
		1908.	1909.	1910.	1911.
Workers.	Number of girls working at the beginning of the year –	18.	11.	7.	6.
	Number of girls working at the end of the year –	11.	7.	6.	10.

Went later in the afternoon to see old Mackay, General Merchant – a tremendous Radical – an interesting old man – very violent for the improvement of his fellow-Highlanders – & a great supporter of the Clan Mackay Society –

I asked him if he knew of any kindred Societies in Canada, thinking they might be useful for Miss Myra Warrand & he said he would 'look up' some addresses – gave me the address of the Church of Scotland & U.F. Church Offices in Edinburgh (so in the evening I wrote to the Secretaries of both of them asking for the names of Highland Ministers out in Canada)

He complained he gets customers who want handknitted socks & stockings & can't get anyone to knit them – So I told him he should write to Miss Macdonald Kilmuir Teacher – & he said he will, but I don't know what prices he will offer –

I also got the names of two Merchants one in Dornie, Loch Duich – & the other at Kyle of Lochalsh whom he says sell hand knitted Hose to him! to retail – very good knitting – the best there is – poor workers – fancy their things going through the hands of two of the small merchants before finding a home.

Mackay is an authority on Clan Tartans – has an immense book of them which is most interesting – he showed it all to me, in fact gave me a regular lecture on the subject in his funny little office upstairs over the shop – sloping roof – huge fire – very oily lamps & a high desk where this book lay – so high it was on a level with my chin! besides a large pattern of every modern Tartan, he has quite a number of most delightful old homespun ones – I've never seen so many before – some so fine they are more like linen – & some Historical pieces such as a bit of the plaid worn by Lord Tullibardine at Culloden & a bit of Niel Gow's Plaid.

Niel Gow's Lament for the Death of his Second Wife is one of the most haunting fiddle tunes ever composed, and still played by accomplished fiddle players today. Born near Dunked in 1727, his father was a weaver of plaid. He had his portrait painted by Henry Raeburn, and in the nineteenth Century, Valentine's of Dundee published a postcard of him which was widely circulated. In Raeburn's portrait he is wearing a dark bluish coat and vest with grey buttons, knee breeches and hose of red and green tartan on a yellowish brown back-ground.

Friday 1st Nov.

Wet – In the afternoon went to see the Basket-Workroom with Miss Cameron – only one of the girls came, & she was a beginner – but they showed me all the materials & more baskets & trays –

Two of the workers are girls attending the 'Secondary' School – both very poor & this work gives them quite enough money to be a real help – I should say they can make as much by it as if they were Knitting Stockings – & can do it at home just in the same way –

The little Workroom is used for the class where there are learners also for storing materials & surplus baskets – but it's only a tiny wooden shed & very cold – so, in the winter Miss Cameron usually takes the girls to her own house.

Mr. Fraser told me, that without her the Industry would have collapsed long ago – She insists on the baskets being up to a certain standard, packs them, invents new shapes, teaches new pupils – they are a very shifting class – as they leave Portree to go to service & that sort of thing, just when they have become really good –

But both Miss Cameron & Mr. Fraser say the work has been a real help in many cases.

Saturday 2nd. Nov.

Lovely day – Wrote all the morning – lunched at the Lodge & played golf in the afternoon –

The Portree Golf Club was opened by Lady Macdonald on July 19th 1899. Scotland had a passion for golf which was helpful in establishing the hand knitting stocking trade in fancy hose. Golf was commonly played by women and men in many different social circles and popularly portrayed by the monarchy and nobility.

Lady Macdonald is anxious to start a sort of "Happy Evening Society or Club" for the boys & girls who are in Portree School – from a distance, nearly all from the Outer Isles, – they live in lodgings & no one takes much interest in them –

The idea is to have classes for piping & dancing for boys – & knitting sewing, & if possible, spinning for girls – The *Comunn Gàidhealach* has sent a singing master this Winter to form a Gaelic Choir & a number of these children have joined it – their ages vary from 14 to 18.

If a knitting & spinning class could be found it might be part of their scheme – the Council paying for the Teacher – as Funds will be the difficulty –

By that time I should have heard from the Minister's wife in the Isle of Berneray, Harris, whether there is any prospect of a class there – as the £10 won't really go very far – but if Berneray falls through Portree might take it's place – & if not some other way of paying the Teacher must be thought out. But all this will come into next months diary. On Monday the Headmaster Mr. Gillanders is to come to the Lodge to talk it over.

	Travelling, Stationery & Postage Expenses from Oct. 27th. to November 3rd. 1912.	£	s.	d.
	carried forward	15.	16.	8
Hiring.	Tip stableman, U.F. Manse, Kilmuir		1.	
	Motor-Coach Uig to Scorrybreck, Portree.		4.	
Stationery.	Envelopes.		1	2 ½
	Labels (for knitted goods for Canada)			2.
Telegrams.	Postmaster Dunvegan			6.
	do Broadford			6.
	Miss Myra Warrand (answer to one from her about the packing etc of the Canadian Tweeds)		1.	6.
Post-cards.	Miss M. Warrand (2)			1.
	Annie Macdonald, Teacher, Kilmuir.			½
	Hon. Sec. (2)			1.
	Sec. *An Comunn Gàidhealach*			½
	Telling Workers about the Edinburgh Sale (8) (This should have been in the accounts a fortninght ago)			4.
Letters.	Miss M. Warrand (3)			3.
	Lady Marjory MacKenzie			1.
	Hon. Sec. (4)			4.
	Miss Morison, U.F. Manse, Clachan, N. Uist.			1.
	William MacKay Esq. Inverness			1.
	Mrs Gillies, U.F. Manse, Clachan, N. Uist.			1.
	John MacPherson, Northbay, Barra.			1.
	Mrs Stewart-MacKenzie.			1.
	E. Maxtone Graham Esq.			1.
	Sec. Church of Scotland Offices. Edinburgh.			1.
	do U.F. Church do do			1.
	MacKenzie, Factor, Dunvegan (2)			2.
	Mrs Patten-MacDougall			1.
	Stewart, Weaver, Benbecula.			2.
	Knitters about Canadian order (8)			8.
	Miss Murray, Lairg Sutherland (order for Forbes Plaid)			1.
	Postage of 2 Parcels of wool from Mrs Hamilton-Campbell.			9.
		16.	9.	6.

Sunday 3rd. to Sunday 10th. November.1912.
(Portree – Broadford Isle of Skye).

Sunday 3rd. Nov.

Wrote diary & letters – lunched at the Lodge – Afterwards walked along the "New Road" with Miss Macdonald & Mrs Bacon (an artist & my fellow-lodger!) – it's the road I had seen the other end of at Staffin & which is not quite finished – it goes through most lovely scenery – Mrs Bacon was very grateful for our protection from the "wild" Highland cattle who struck fear to her heart – although she would like to paint them & although her maiden name was MacAlpin.

Monday 4th. Nov.

Wet – wrote – In the afternoon went up to the Lodge – Gillanders, Headmaster, was there (he comes from Maryburgh, Ross-shire – but has been 35 years at the Portree School) – & was very anxious that Lady Macdonald's plan for helping the children should come to pass – there are 91 children – about 60 girls & 30 boys – of ages from 14 to 18. – most of them are very friendless & not too well fed or comfortable in their lodgings – They decided to call a meeting & form a Committee on Thursday afternoon.

There seems to be no one who would or could teach Knitting – Wrote to Miss Lockhart, Struan (12 miles from Portree) who has been recommended as the best knitter in Skye – & asked if there is any chance that she would be able to come in & give lessons to a class.

Went, late, to tea with Miss Cameron (the Basket-Teacher) She is the daughter of a famous former Fiscal of Lochmaddy – & gives Music-lessons at something like 15/- a quarter! as well as the basket work –

Tuesday 5th. Nov.

The usual rain – wrote all this morning – Had a message from Mr. Fraser (Baskets-Solicitor) asking if I could come & see him in the afternoon – went to his office at 4. – he gave me his Report to Dr. Scott (The Congested Districts Enquiries) to copy for the Council –

Also the following figures on the price of wool – taken from the accounts of a farm which his Firm have the management of: –

Blackfaced Wool (sold in Leith by Wool-Brokers).

year	
1906.	it sold at 8d. per lb. (16/- the stone)
1911.	" " " 7¼d." " (14/6 " ").

and has been as low as 5¼d. or 10/- per stone.

Then in the
Transactions of the Highland Agricultural Society
(Vol. XXIV p. 373.)

White Highland Wool. (This is black-faced he says) sold at from 13/- to 14/6. per stone.
(This is down in my note-book, but I don't remember if it was quoted at the price per lb. or per stone – the latter I imagine as that is how I noted it down) –
These figures are all calculated on a stone of wool containing 24lb. which I was told several times in Uist is correct – but I used to think a stone was 28. lbs. Mr. Fraser didn't seem to know – so took my word for it being 24. –
However if it is really 28. then the price in 1906. was 18/8. not 16/-.

Note:
Have since been told that the old "Highland" Stone is 24. bls. but the "English" stone is 14 lbs.
Only in the Outer Isles is the Highland Measure still used.

The following was given me when in Benbecula by Margaret Macdonald, Griminish.

(copy.). Receipted Bill by D. MacTavish on behalf of the Scottish Home Industries at Creagorry. Benbecula. 9th. June. 1912.

	Item	£	s.	d.
9 ½ d per lb.	1 stone Grogorry Wool (name of a S. Uist Farm).		19	0.
11½ per lb.	1/2 stone _______? wool at 23/-		11	6.
	1 Boll Flour		18	0.
	1 Bar Soap			9.
	1 lb Tea		1	10.
	1/2 Boll _______? (Indian Meal?)		10	0.
		3.	1.	1.

(The items are written in pencil & very faint but all the figures are quite distinct.)

	£	s.	d.
With this wool she made 30 yards of Tweed for which she received 2/9 per yd. =	4.	2.	6.

But to make this web she had to pay out as follows: –

	£	s	d
For wool –	1.	10.	6.
do weaving		9.	0.
do carding		4.	8.
do freight of carded wool		1.	2.
do soap			9.
do dyes		2.	0.
	2.	8.	1.
Price received for finished web.	4.	2.	6.
Cost of producing do do	2.	8.	1.
Profit on the do do	1.	14.	5.
But of this profit she had already spent	1.	9.	10.
Leaving in actual money to spend –		4.	7.

The figures for weaving – carding – & dyes
are what she told me – she said nothing
about food for the women who did the working.

The same women gave me the following prices
of dyes: –

Copper (or copperas)	2d.	per	lb.
Logwood	2d.	"	"
Redwood	2d.	"	"
Indigo	6d.	"	oz.
Alum	2d.	"	lb.

2oz. indigo will dye light blue 4 or 5lbs wool –
2.lbs. Alum, required for 2 lb. green or yellow wool.

Mrs MacLean, Carnan Inn, S. Uist told me the following: –

1. stone of wool makes about 15 yds Tweed. ⅓ weight of wool is lost in the cleaning (& in throwing away what is useless for spinning).

Copy of D. MacTavish's letter in answer to mine enquiring about prices –

Scottish Home Industries Association
Lochmaddy. 12 Sept. 1912

"....................The highest price we pay for Tweeds just now is 2/10. per yd – we give 2/11. for crotals (solid) & the lowest price 2/9. per yd. : As our trade is purely a wholesale trade, I believe at the present time tweeds are being sold to the wholesale houses at less than cost. But, at the best, the wholesale house only gives about 3/- to 3/1. per yd. for our tweeds.

At some of the Duchess's sales I am told that the price is 5/- to 5/9. per yd. This must be done to cover cost of sale & to satisfy the wholesale houses & without those big buyers we could not keep the Industry going.

In fact our Association never paid a fraction of dividend to their Directors.

We charge 20/- per stone for Ewe & Hog Wool.

I always refuse a tweed that is bad – & it is a very exceptional case that we pay less than 2/9.

For tweeds sold in suit lengths over the counter here we charge 3/6 to 4/- per yd. – but this again is to keep the wholesale right –

If the wholesale could be got rid of & a large Society formed with plenty of Capital to sell the tweed, I believe the price would go up to the worker.

....

....Yours faithfully
D. MacTavish.

Another fact vouched for by Mr. Fraser is, that goods go cheaper by Steamer from Glasgow to America than from Glasgow to Portree!

Wednesday. 6th. Nov.

Very wet – & very warm – Wrote – went to tea at "Viewfield" with the Harry Macdonald's – Miss Macdonald takes a great interest in Knitting – showed me a golf-jersey Knitted by "Mrs" Lockhart who is sister of their cook – & says she works them for Chalmers' of Oban – & she thinks gets a fairly good price from him – I got the names from her of various Knitters who send things to the local show.

Thursday 7th. Nov.

Another pouring wet day & very warm too –

Went to help Macdonalds' Meeting about the "Happy Evenings" – a number of people present & it was decided to form an Association, with membership for the boys & girls who will pay 1/- a year to belong to it.

Unable to settle anything definite about the Knitting class or spinning either – but hope it may be managed once the Happy Evenings have started going –

Had a letter from Miss Lockhart in the evening saying she could not undertake to teach.

Had tea at "Redcliff" with the John Macdonalds – their sister in law Mrs Scott from Erisay, Harris, was there too – & she told me a little about Obbe, Harris, where I hope to go next year.

Packed in the evening for the early start next day.

Friday 8th. Nov.

Left Portree 7.a.m. Steamer (the "*Glencoe*"), arrived Broadford, Campbell's Hotel, about 9. o'clock. – after breakfast – saw the Proprietor, Campbell, & he said he was going up to the Marble Quarries in the motor & would I like to come – so I went – it's about 5 miles off – & was very wet – so was a splendid opportunity of getting there in comfort!

Saw "Nairne" the manager – the works & quarries are all closed, indefinitely, but – may start again if more money can be got!

There is marble of every variety of colour & veining, or whatever the right word may be – We saw the actual quarries only in the distance – up on the hillside – 6 or 7 of them – looking like ordinary stone ones only white –

Near the "Works" outside – are dozens of large slabs – standing on end like numbers of tombstones in rows –

Inside in an enormous place like a Railway Station, we saw all the slumbering machinery – looking reproachfully at us – deserted machinery can look so sad –

The Manager leant up against an iron pillar – stuck his thumbs into his waistcoat arm holes & aired his views on the Highland, or Skye Character – Mr. Campbell of the Hotel only restraining himself from flying at his throat, then & there, by a great effort.

The Manager is a more lowland body who however calls himself a "cosmopo-lee-taine" as he has lived in Spain & other vague foreign parts – he looks the part in riding breeches & a white corduroy jacket with astrachan collar & cuffs –

He says that in the quarries boys of from 15 expected "man's" wages & got it – & grumbled that men left off early in the afternoon in order to go & help their wives with the crofts. – or didn't come at all sometimes – as they had potatoes to lift or corn to cut – Laughed heartily at the idea of a boy holding a class for other boys for carving in marble – but his opinions changed in such a " cosmopolitaine" way during the course of conversation that he reminded me of the "lightning calculator" I once saw at the Hippodrome – he ended by saying that the marble is there " for the taking" – all the rubbish – some very good lumps – & waste chips – enough to last the boys for years.

After luncheon called on the Lamonts, Church of Scotland Manse, but he was out – had a talk with her – & heard there are a number of Knitters in the District.

Then went onto the School – but, MacPherson the Headmaster, had closed rather early as the *Comunm Gàidhealach* Choir was going to a concert in Isleornsay, I think, – left a message & note for him.

Called at a house opposite & saw one of the only spinners left in Broadford– a very nice Mrs MacInnes – (native of Kilmuir), She loves her wheel – also Knitting – makes yarn & knits every kind of under-garment for herself & her husband – I told her Of Mrs Pattie MacDougall's offer to sell yarn – & she was very pleased & will make some to send –

After "supper" Rev. Lamont came in to see me – then says the boys love their carving class & the reason they sent none of their work to St Andrews, was, that they had sold all they had – just at a local bazaar – & then at Lady Ann Murray's Industry Sale at Kyle of Lochalsh (unless it was at a Sale at Plockton – have got rather mixed between these two sales I've vaguely heard of – they may be one & the same)

The class is advertised to re-open for the Winter in the School on Monday evening at seven o'clock, – so I shall go & see it.

The Rev Lamont has offered to give up the whole of Monday to taking me to see people who knit – & one Weaveress about 3 miles off in Breakish.

Mr. Lamont is a Canadian Born & seems to be very energetic, they say he is a very fine Gaelic preacher & has a large congregation – as at the "Disruption" this parish had a strong Minister Dr. MacKinnon who kept his people – & they have been kept ever since – he & the U.F. Minister Mr. MacLeod, are great friends & ready to work together.

The Free Church of Scotland is a Presbyterian Church adhering in its worship and doctrine to the position adopted by the Church of Scotland at the Reformation. Its divergence from the body known as the Church of Scotland dates from the Disruption of 1843 when, under the leadership of Dr Thomas Chalmers, the Evangelical Party in the Church of Scotland as by Law Established, withdrew from the Establishment to form the Church of Scotland, Free.

Saturday 9th Nov.

Very stormy & wet – waves dashing over the Pier in the morning –

Started walking after luncheon – called first on Rev MacLeod – a Lewisman – he is very interested in every Industry including the Marble class which he says is a good thing for the boys – & a real "home" industry for winter evenings – not as a great means of making money, but as an "addition" – He will help about knitting & would like to see spinning revived. (I don't feel very hopeful of this, in a place like Broadford – which is almost a town in a way – but in the outlying townships it might be possible)

Rev MacLeod & Rev Lamont will have a meeting for me about the work on Tuesday evening in the Reading Room – to choose a Committee & someone to do this "writing" on the same lines as in Kilmuir –

Mr. MacLeod is also going to write to some of his friends in Canada about Miss Warrand & the tweeds –

We discussed the "fraudulent tweed" of the Lewis – The present system he referred to as a form of "sweating" & thinks the people right in many ways to make what will bring in the most money – as the real stuff brings in so miserably little – This sounds as if he were an aggressive sort of person – but this is not the case at all – he was exceedingly nice about it & is mainly anxious that the women should get proper pay for their work – in some ways he thinks the tweed industry has done harm in the Islands – it has made the men depend too much on their wives earnings – & caused extra laziness among them!

Went next to see Miss Campbell (the Hotel mans' sister) she lives with her mother & 2 other brothers who have a shop. I asked her to come to the meeting & be on the Committee – she will – but I don't fancy is inclined to do much – unlike her brother of the Hotel who will also be one of the Committee & help to sell their things to Tourists who constantly demand stockings & tweeds.

Next called on Miss Gollan, U.F. Lady Worker (same thing as Miss Russel & Miss Kirk) – she is most ready to help – & will take me on Tuesday morning to see some people – & on Wednesday she wants me to go to a Township called Elgoll 16 miles away where there is still much spinning & the people are very poor & in need of help – so settled to drive there with her –

Promised to call & see Mrs Leah at Corry Lodge – (Caretaker – Lady Macdonald's servant) on Sunday afternoon as this Miss Gollan vouched for her not minding the day! & says she is splendid about anything of that kind.

Have settled to stay in Broadford till Friday 15th. Nov & then go to Strath, Gairloch, Ross-shire, & possibly end by a visit to Inverbroom, Ullapool, if Lady Fowler can have me –

Slabs of Marble stacked on the Platform of the Marble-Quarry-Station. (the only Railway in the Isle of Skye) The "Snow Effect" is from the powdered White Marble.

	Travelling – Stationery – & Postage Expenses from Sunday 3rd. to Sunday 10th. Nov. 1912.			
	Carried Forward	16.	9.	6.
Hiring.	"Machine" Scorrybreck to the Pier, Portree		3.	0.
	porters		1.	0.
	Tip to boy at Scorrybreck (for posting letters late every night).		1.	0.
Steamer.	Portree to Broadford –		3.	6.
Stationery	Envelopes			2.
Postcards.	Broadford Postmaster			½
	Broadford hotel (Campbell's)			½
Letters.	Mrs Burnley Campbell			1.
	Mrs. Watson, Strath, Gairloch.			1.
	Miss Lockhart, Struan, Skye.			1.
	Hon. Sec. (2)			2.
	Miss M. Warrand (3)			3.
	Mrs. Macdonald, Post Office, Isle of Berneray.			1.
	Alex. Stewart, Weaver, Benbecula.			1.
	Lady Fowler, Inverbroom.			1.
	Duncan Davidson of Tulloch (about willows)			1.
		16.	19.	2.

Young Outer Islanders (at Clachan, North Uist)
(6 children in outer clothing)

Sunday 10th. to Sunday 17th. October. 1912. (Broadford Isle of Skye – Gairloch Ross-shire)

Sunday 10th Nov.

Wet – wrote diary & letters – In the evening went to see Mrs Leah, caretaker at Corry Lodge – She will be very pleased to help in any way she can, about the Industries – used to be very fond of spinning in her young days but has no time for it now – she thinks her daughter Louie would like to go in for it –

Mrs Leah is a native of Sutherland, & her husband is English (gamekeeper) – she is U.F. & a great friend of Miss Gollan's.

Monday 11th Nov.

Very wet – very cold & a tremendous wind – the high tops of Applecross on the mainland covered with fresh snow –

Went for a long round with Rev. Lamont, starting after breakfast & getting back in the dark – Walked a good 10 miles which seemed like twenty! because of the high wind, & having to walk in oilskins.

We went first to the last weaver in the district, or rather, Weaveress – one "Eirig" MacKenzie – at Ashaig – A queer little wooden hut – the last house in the Township right on the edge of the moor – the minister told me "It was on just such a day as this, last year, that an old man came to a funeral, & on the way home wandered away away on the hill (waving his hand beyond the wooden hut of Eirig) & was lost, – & it was on just such a day as this that we went to his funeral".

This story may have depressed me & may be the reason why Eirig was more depressing still! Her hut new & painted bright yellow seemed out of harmony with the landscape – Mr. Lamont said he'd not been to see her since she got into her new house – & then I felt pretty certain she would not have moved her loom with her – that yellow hut simply couldn't hold a loom! – & nor it did – she had broken it up – she, herself proved to be rather a short square very masculine looking lady & most forbidding – with a hooked nose & gruff voice – the inside of the yellow house more like a Canadian "Shack" than a Highland Croft – an American stove & pipe – all very new – & all rough & comfortless & ugly – she has a brother living with her – still has her spinning-wheel which she reluctantly fetched from an inner room & the Minister persuaded her to sit down & spin – which she did – but very badly – & she has no wish to have anything to do with Home-Industries – The Minister made her unearth an old Quern (*Bràth*) for grinding corn – but she no longer uses it & has lost half of it – It was a horrid little hut & I, for one, was cold & tired & felt my heart sliding down into my Norwegian boots which are very good for keeping the wet out – but very heavy to walk far in!

We next walked a mile or so 'cross country' – down to the sea – & visited some

MacPhersons in a thatched house – The hostess, a grumbling kind of person – spins a little but hasn't taught her daughter Jessie – a nice bright girl of about 16. who is very fond of Knitting – the mother told me she had another wheel an old one which she doesn't use – so, remembering that Mrs Burnley Campbell wants wheels for her spinning-class, I asked if it was for sale – & she said yes, & went & fetched it – dirty & in very bad order – been patched up with rough bits of deal – but might have been made to work – I asked if she would take 15/- for it – (worth about 10/- really) & she indignantly said she had refused £2. for it – that it belonged to her "5th grandmother, & was very great relic of olden days" – so then I told her I thought it was far too valuable to part with. – after that she took no further interest in me – Jessie the girl would like to sell some of her knitted work during the winter.

The next croft was of a very different type – Macphersons too – but such a nice cheery happy family – a father, mother, & daughter 'Bella' – new stone house – the cleanest & most comfortable I've seen for ages – Mrs. spins & Bella Knits – they have a Quern too & got a sheaf of corn & showed me how it was worked – & we went outside & I Kodaked first her & then him working it – they still use it sometimes, but when he was a little boy, it was always used – & if a stranger came to the house a sheaf of corn would be brought in & meal ground & baked & eaten before he left the place –

After the Kodaking we were given some tea & scones very reviving –

In April 1912,the Eastman Kodak Company of Rochester, New York, introduced a vest-pocket folding camera. It is possible that this was the camera Isabell used to take her photographs.

I was feeling pretty well dead-beat – In walking along Mr. Lamont was very nice & kept on saying "now you must just be regulating the pace yourself Miss MacKenzie", but, all the same he was always one step in front of me – & nothing is more tiring than continually trying to catch up a person!

From there on had a stiff walk across swampy ground uphill to the road again.

Called at Breakish School – but it & the house both shut up – Broadford school also closed – It was after 5 by the time we got there – Next to the Broadford Hotel where we saw Mrs MacInnes who will help – & be on the Industry Committee – a very nice woman – Established Church – Then called to see Rev MacLeod for a minute – & he said he will be at the meeting on Tuesday – Mr Lamont has to go to Inverness so won't be able to come –

The last bit of the homeward way the wind dead against us again –

Meant to go & see the Marble class at 8. p.m – but so tired gave up the idea.

Mrs Ian MacPherson
Crofter's wife, Lower Breakish, Skye,
grinding corn in the
Quern, (Gaelic "*Bràth*").

Tuesday 12th Nov

More stormy than yesterday – hail & snow storms & a tremendous "sea" –

Had an appointment in the morning to visit people with Miss Gollan the U.F. Lady Worker – struggled as far as her house, near the post-office & then did a number of visits with her –

Saw one woman who is half paralyzed but can use her hands (when she is alone & wants to move across the room she crawls on her hands) & supports herself by knitting – socks for men & stockings for women – she is a widow & her daughter & twin grandchildren, boys of 6. live with her, the daughter who was married to an Irishman has been deserted by him.

It's such a dear little room – whitewashed with tiny bright blue blobs of whitewash (or bluewash if there is such a thing –) dashed on the walls at regular intervals of about, a foot apart – the whole effect reminded one of white cups & saucers with a blue pattern one so often sees in cottages – it was the daughter's idea – the mother so cheery & tidy with a piece of black satin ribbon tied over her head & under her chin – like a black "mutch".

In another town next door there was a much sadder case – a poor bed-ridden woman – tied into knots with rheumatism & looking most dreadfully ill – been in bed something like15 years – her sister who looks after her is a good knitter – there is a funny old pauper lodger "Mary" who can knit socks & used to spin but has no wheel now.

Went to the school & saw MacPherson the headmaster & the teachers Miss Cameron & Miss Turnbull – they will come to the meeting – I asked, whether, in the event of getting up a spinning class, the Inner room in the school would be available & heard it would & that the wheels could be left there quite well.

Called too on Mrs MacInnes (my original spinning friend in Broadford) & asked whether she would be prepared to teach a spinning class if we had one, & she said she would be very glad to – living exactly opposite the school & being a good spinner she seems just the right person.

Got back to the Hotel by 2 o'clock & didn't go out again till the evening – storm continued – & the Mail Boat being unable to get into the Pier, rolled past taking all our letters on to Portree –

Hired a dogcart & drove to the meeting, taking Mrs Leah with me – offered to take Mrs Lamont, but she had friends with her & couldn't come at all – I was sorry as I wanted her to be there & become "Convenor" of the Committee for Home Industries in Broadford or rather in the parish of Strath –

It was such a bad night it was very doubtful whether any people would turn up or not – but quite a number came, including several boys of the marble class & their Teacher Donald Cameron. It was in the Reading room, such a cosy place – big fire – good lamps & lots of books & tables –

Mr. MacLeod just talked about the Industries & then I explained a little about what we want to do in Broadford – knitting & spinning & the marble-carving –

We elected a Committee with Mrs Lamont as convenor – & the teacher Miss Turnbull & Mrs Leah as joint secretaries –

For the spinning -class, four school-girls of about 14 – then 2 teachers, Miss Gollan & Louie Leah all said they wanted to learn – so arranged to have it three times a week (subject to the Council's approval) on alternate nights to the marble-carving class.

In 1910 Mrs Burnley Campbell established a marble carving class at Broadford, this was part of the attempt to introduce income for the islanders.The Skye Osier Company was also started at Kilmuir, a collaboration between the Home Industries Board and the Congested District Board.

– There was asked if girls would be allowed to join the marble class – & said I thought they might, provided that Donald Cameron would undertake to teach so many (ten girls including the 2 teachers wanted to join it) – & also if the tools could be got from the Council. – it seems the girls have been longing to join it for over a year –

Wrote to the Hon. Sec. same evening & asked about this.

Wednesday 13th Nov.

Had arranged to drive to the Township of Elgol 15 miles away, with Miss Gollan, – but so cold & stormy I gave it up.

Wrote letters & didn't go out till after tea. Then went to see Miss Gollan – & after that Mrs MacInnes to talk more about the spinning class – wheels may be a difficulty in some cases – they are hard to get – I have a spare one at Kilcoy & will send it for the use of one Morag MacPherson a motherless girl of about 15, who has an invalid father, & who will always have to stay at home – so she is the very girl who should learn to spin & knit – if she really takes to the work I will give her the wheel out-right – Perhaps some of the Council may have a spare wheel or two ? !

Went on then to the Marble-Carving-Class. 8 o'clock instead of 7.30. as Donald is the "Post" & the boat had been late –

Nine boys in the class & a tenth without any tools – all looking full of happiness & intent on what they wanted to do – the Schoolmaster was there too – helping to manage everything – this was really the "Beginning" class – as – at the one on Mon. nothing could be done as they had forgotten to get any marble! so, after all, it's a good thing I didn't go.

They were very busy so I stayed only a short time as Donald is shy & was evidently rather embarassed by my being there & watching his first efforts at teaching –

Each boy had a small slice of marble & a heavy little iron mallet & set of chisels without handles – the thing that struck me most was the extreme wobblyness of the old school desks they had to work on – half the power of a stroke must be lost owing to this.

Also the lighting was so bad – a couple of wall lamps (the kind with reflectors) poised on upturned packing cases between the 2 rows of desks – some of the boys almost in darkness – It seems there are two larger hanging lamps but they are out of order & MacPherson said he is "going to send them to be repaired"

It was very dark walking home, but Miss Gollan kindly came all the way with me.

Thursday 14th Nov.

Much warmer – & a mist – calm sea once more –

Wrote all the morning – After lunch called on Mrs Lamont & told her all about the Committee – classes etc – she is a plump cheery little soul with a face like a russet apple – & is very willing to help & says she will have a meeting of the Committee after Xmas to see how they are all getting on & what has been done –

Mr. Lamont was returning by the Steamer so she begged me to come in on my way home & see him.

Went to the school – the choir sang some of their Gaelic songs delightfully, they won second prize at the Mod this year – the first time they had ever competed & were very pleased – Miss Cameron, who trained them, talked about the Mod – her whole face glowed with pleasure & she said they had The Week of their lives – like Fairyland –

An Comunn Gàidhealach founded in Oban in 1891, organises and runs the Royal National Mod and a network of provincial mods every year, to promote, support and develop Gaelic language and Culture.

MacPherson said he feared Donald Cameron would not be able to teach 10 girls as well as 10 boys – as only 4 of these boys are old pupils, the rest quite beginners – the girls are very disappointed – I said that perhaps after Christmas when the boys will have got beyond the first stages of the work, some of the girls might then join – especially the 2 teachers – as next year they could help to teach real beginners themselves –

I also asked whether it would not be possible for some of them to get up an entertainment to raise money for buying a good stout table or bench to work at.

Called an another Mrs MacInnes who has a wee wee shoppie of sweeties & paraffin & matches & soups & there may be tea & sugar but I don't think anything else – her daughter Annie aged 14, is to be one of the spinners – the mother is so pleased at the idea of her learning – she comes from Dunvegan & her own mother is a beautiful spinner but never allowed her "to put a finger on the wheel" & so she never learnt – but she has no wheel for Annie (the mother in Dunvegan having now given hers to another daughter who uses it) – I said that at first she could share mine with Morag as one can card half the time while the other spins & vice versa –

In the Winter the class will card & spin & in the summer Mrs MacInnes will take them out to get heather, crottal, etc. & they will the do the whole process of dyeing the wool –

This spinning-class is being started because I found they really want to learn – so I hope it will be successful – I think it was lucky coming across Mrs MacInnes – a simple, gentle old fashioned Highland woman – who has no children & a husband whom I am afraid drinks a good deal sometimes – everyone speaks well of her – She it was who told me about little Morag MacPherson who lives near her & she "keeps an eye on her" as she has no mother.

Saw Mr. Lamont on the way home – he is very glad about the classes & hopes one day to get a weaver in the district – perhaps next year a boy might be taught and helped to get a loom.

Ended the walk with another visit to Mrs Leah. she is busy "sorting" her old wheel for Louie.

We agreed how beautiful the Sutherland Tweeds are – & she was awfully pleased when I said that of all the Tweeds from all over Scotland at the St. Andrews sale, the Sutherland ones were the best.

Friday 15th Nov.

The Steamer was supposed to leave Broadford at 8.30. a.m. went on board – but were delayed a long time by Highland Cows who couldn't be induced to come on board. – three times after they had been coaxed by the whole crew of the "Glencoe" & all the loafers on the Pier & the 'Herd' in charge of them, as far as the gangway – did they whirl round, flourish their horns in the faces of their tormentors & broke through in a wild stampede till they were brought up short by the Pier gates – at last they were roped round the horns, two men tugging at the end of the ropes – two or three more twisting their tails & others prodding them with prickly brooms – all shouting down the gangway they were pulled and thrust, – poor beasts. one was so sorry for them & felt there ought to have been a Home-Secretary or someone to grant them a reprieve at the last minute – as a reward for their plucky fight.

It was very wet – so I went down to the "saloon" Where I was caught by Miss Russell the U.F. Lady Worker in Isleornsay (met her at Kilmuir.) who was on her way back there & was recovering from "Flue" & filling the place with fumes of eucalyptus – had to talk for a long time – till I fled on deck for a breath of fresh air with the excuse of wanting to look after my luggage – & forgot to return.

Took the train from Kyle of Lochalsh To Achnasheen, a tiresome old porter would insist On weighing my luggage – & confirmed it was more than 60.lbs.

At Achnasheen time for a hasty lunch before the coach started for Gairloch – a drizzling mist the whole way, but in spite of it Loch Maree still continued to look beautiful

Arrived Gairloch Hotel about 6.30 & got a one horse sleay to take me on to Strath.

Saturday 16th Nov.

Lovely day (naturally! – being – Ross-shire)

After lunch walked over to call at the MacAskills (he is Sir Kenneth MacKenzie's Factor) – as Lady Marjory had said he would be able to give me a good deal of information about the Knitters in the different districts – and he was most useful – Lady Marjory having already discussed with him her plans for re-organizing the Knitting Industry in Gairloch.

He also cleared up the Wool mystery – it seems the 24. lb. stone is the old Highland or Scottish Measure which was in use before the Union – & everywhere now except in the Outer Isles the English measure of the 14lb. stone is used! – this, of course explains exactly the extraordinary difference in price that rules on the West side & east side of the Minch – it seems Sir Kenneth's Shepherd at Flourdale still 'thinks' in Highland stones that's how Mr.MacAskill knows it so well – but he was surprised to hear its always used in the Outer Isles –

The Agents for the two Associations use it. I suppose they gave up, or never tried getting the people to understand the 14lb one. After all they use both most easily & happily in their lineal measure, the Highland yard to pay the Weaver! & the English yard to get paid for the Tweed! The Highland yard makes a yard & a quarter of the English!

In future I shall do all my wool 'problems' at so much a lb.

	Travelling – Stationery – Postage – Expenses from Nov. 10th. to Nov. 17th. 1912.	£	s	d
	Carried forward,	16.	19.	2.
Travelling.	Dogcart (going to Broadford Industry Meeting)		3	0.
	Steamer, Broadford to Kyle of Lochalsh –		2.	0.
	Train Kyle of Lochalsh to Achnasheen.		3.	0.
	Overweight Luggage		1.	6.
	Coach Achnasheen to Gairloch –		9.	0.
	"Machine" Gairloch Hotel to Strath		2.	6.
	Porters – whole journey –		2.	0.
Stationery.	2 Reams Writing-paper & postage (1 Ream 2/6 one 3/6)		6.	10.
Telegram.	Gairloch Post office (from Broadford about forwarding letters).			6.
Postcard.	Gairloch Post office.			½
	To all the post-offices in the Islands where stray letters may be lying (8).			4.
Letters.	Hon. Sec. (4).			4
	Mrs Watson, Strath.			1.
	Mrs. Macdonald, U.F. Manse Kilmuir.			1.
	Annie Macdonald, Teacher, Kilmuir			1.
	Factor, Dunvegan (2)			2.
	A. Ross, Edinburgh.			1.
	Miss Campbell, Kilberry. (sent her pair hose made from her pattern in Barra – want her opinion on them).			1½
		18.	10.	10.
	Carried forward	18.	10.	10.
Letters (Continued)	Lexie Macleod, South Uist,			1.
	Type-writing Co (order for paper)			1.
	Mrs Burnley-Campbell (2).			2.
	Mrs Lachlan Morrison, N. Uist			1.
	Mrs Morrison, U.F. Manse, Isle of Berneray.			1.
	Rev. MacLeod, U.F. Manse, Broadford.			1.
	Sec. An Comunn Gaidhealach			1.
	Mrs MacLaren, ledaig, Argyll.			1.
	Lady Marjory MacKenzie			1.
		18.	11.	8.

Sunday 17th. Nov. to Sunday 8th. Dec. 1912.
Gairloch Inverbroom Kilcoy.

Monday 18th. to Sat 22nd.

From Monday 18th. till Sat 22nd. I spent most of the time getting through a great deal of writing – long arrears of the card-index to bring up to date besides a fair number of letters to answer – and sorting-out letters about orders sent through the Council for tweed and knitted things & entering them in a book.

Had two interviews with the MacIntyre sisters Maggie and Tina – Maggie teaches in the school & Tina helps in the shop & looks after the house, so they are very busy and are most anxious to go on with the work their mother did among the Knitters in Gairloch – She used to get all the orders carried out for Lady MacKenzie & send them off to the shop at Strathpeffer & to the Highland Home Industries Show at Inverness. – Knew each worker personally & the quality of their work – this I have often heard from Lady Marjory who rather feared the daughters might not have time to go on with it.

But they are very keen to enter into any new scheme Lady Marjory may propose for enlarging the amount of work done in the district, & although they don't know as much about it as their mother they know a great deal. They each promised to give up their next holiday to coming with me to see some of the best workers – Maggie on Sat. & Tina on Weds. (early closing day in the shop) – however Sat. fell through as I had a cold & it was a bad day – but Maggie came to see me instead & gave me a good deal of information.

She thinks some girls should be encouraged to spin – Gairloch yarn is splendid but there is not enough of it – they are sending a fair quantity at present to Chalmers of Oban who gives from 9d. to 10d. a cut for it – a much better price than he offered for the stockings – the Gairloch people like all others whom I have asked, will not make them for his price (3/- to 3/3 per pair – this includes the yarn spun & dyed at home)

Then also there are only two women left who can knit the tartan hose which used to be a feature of Gairloch Knitting –

In Achtercairn school (near Strath) where Maggie teaches there are actually no children or only one child, I forgot which she said, who have ever even seen a spinning- wheel! this she discovered quite by accident not long ago – but the district these children come from is, I fancy, not a spinning one at all – the women Knit always with the shop wool –

The women of Sand & Opinan & Point go in for spinning – yarn – not tweed that is made at Inverasdail – but too far off for me to go at this time of year.

Talking about yarn & the Long Highland "hundred" skein – the MacIntyres tell me that Lady MacKenzie has got the people to do their yarn into "shop" skeins & its sold by the cut of two skeins exactly like shop wool – they got short "*cros-iarna*" (winders) made for them & they use these & put 60 threads in a skein like the machine stuff – In a way it seems rather a pity to have done this as the long Highland skein of 100 threads is just about equal to 2 of the English ones of 60. each – but I suppose it is convenient for selling to people who can't understand the long skein!

Lady MacKenzie supplies the shop wool for the stockings she orders & merely pays the women for knitting them – this is a system they seem to prefer – as they have to 'put out' none of their own money – I think the wool comes from the MacIntyres shops & that they keep an account of it.

All the people I talked to about the Knitters & spinners seem to agree that, now poor Mrs MacIntyre is gone, the Industry requires some new life putting into it – & they seem to be waiting for any scheme Lady Marjory may propose –

Monday 24th Nov.

Walked to Sand by myself – about three miles – called first at Little Sand Farm & saw Miss MacGillivray the farmer's sister (quite young) – she showed me the way to a short cut across to most of the crofts – & gave me names of knitters – mostly ones I already had from the MacIntyres – she said she would do anything in the world for Lady Marjory! on hearing I was a friend of hers, insisted that I should return to tea on my way home. – she and her sister knit lovely shetland shawls from their own wool which they got spun by a woman in Sand – & said they would sometimes like to sell them.

After that the first house I went to was that of an oldish Margaret MacPherson who used to do a good deal for Lady MacKenzie, but was very ill lately & is not knitting at present anyway – hers was a new house right on the edge of the sea – she offered to show me the way up to other houses but as she looked very frail I did not allow her to.

Next came to the croft of one Annie Macdonald (the daughter) – Very friendly indeed but frankly announced that the one thing in the world she hates is knitting or spinning – Laundry-work holds a high place in her affections & she had once helped 6 months in lady Marjory's Laundry – she guided me over dykes and fields & stepping -stones to MacKenzie's shoppie & there a namesake of my own gave me a good many more names – mostly duplicate ones.

By that time it was getting dusk so I made my way back to the MacGillivrays & had a hasty tea & hot shortbread & it was dark most of the way back to Strath till the moon rose.

Tuesday 25th Nov.

Paid some unofficial visits! people whom I've known when staying at Flourdale & who would be rather hurt if I'd been in Gairloch without going to see them – Ended by tea at the "Bank" – & was caught in a terrific squall on the way home – fortunately Mrs Burgess had lent me her son Alie to see me home "past the churchyard' (!!) & I was thankful as without his arm to cling to like a drowning man & a plank – I know I should have been thrown straight into the ditch & spent the night there – 2 days later I read of the same squall in the papers, which had visited the rest of Scotland rather earlier in the afternoon – if it went on to the Outer Isles I'm afraid a good many roofs must have been lifted off by it.

Weds. 26th Nov.

This being Tina MacIntyre's half holiday we drove to the other side – Opinan & Point.

South of Gairloch, a single track road travels for eight miles west then south ending at Red Point (*Rua Reidh*, meaning Smooth Point).

Very cold & stormy – when it wasn't snowing it was hailing – At Opinan picked up Mrs MacKenzie (whom Lady Marjory had asked me to see) & she came on with us & took us to see some of the best knitters & spinners at Point which place is the end of all things on the West side –

The yarn spun by these people is like comparing a silk thread with a bit of string to that spun by the women of the Outer Isles – and they make the most beautiful colours – one of the best, quite a young woman, had only taken to it since she married 3 or 4 years ago.

Afterwards in Mrs MacKenzie's own house we saw some more very good knitting – undergarments – she has a great friend in Applecross who is a very good spinner & whose name she gave me too for the Register –

On the way back would have stopped in Badachro but it was really the beginning of the snow storm & there was already about 2 inches on the ground & the man driving us must have been perished with cold during his many waits.

Thursday 28th Nov

Went with Mrs Watson my landlady to see some good knitters in the Lonmore district quite near Strath – these are the people who knit with shop wool – we saw most of the prize winners & all had stockings on hand, beautiful knitting & they are very quick workers.

Friday. 29th. Nov.

Left Strath, Gairloch at 11 am. drove first to Gairloch Hotel where I met the coach – for Achnasheen – reached there about 6. after one of the coldest drives I ever remember – snow on the ground and freezing hard all day. – I watched the faces of my three fellow passengers, men, & the driver turning from red to blue & from blue to violet – & felt my own was probably far worse! they revived themselves with drams at Loch Maree & Kinlochewe Hotels 10 miles interval between each – & I drank hot tea out of my Thermos.

Had an hour to get warm in at Achnasheen before the train for Garve – Slept the night at Garve Hotel.

Saturday 30th Nov.

Lady Fowler kindly sent her motor to fetch me – and we ploughed through the snow to Inverbroom (about 26 miles) after having to "hoot" hinds & once three stags off the road. – More snow fell during the night & then the road became blocked for motor traffic for several days.

> Lady Alice Fowler was an enthusiastic Scottish naturalist, a collector in the field of lepidoptera. her portrait is in the Victoria and Albert Museum, London. She took the initiative to have an archaeological investigation done of the Cairn at Inverlael, near Lochbroom in 1914.

Sunday 1st. Dec to Weds. 4th. Dec.

These days Lady Fowler gave me a very great deal of information & many valuable hints about the management of her Sales etc. & showed me all her books – besides giving me the names and addresses & amount of work done this year by all her workers.

– If the snow had not been so deep, we were to have visited a number of them – but they are all a distance away from Inverbroom so this was impossible.

The Industries are confined to the Parish of Lochbroom (its the second largest in Scotland).

Twenty years ago when Lady Fowler started selling tweeds for the people the Sales amounted to about £30 & now they are close to £300. – they seemed to have reached high water mark 2 years ago – & now are a little less, but this she attributes to the old age pension – old people not requiring to go on working to the very end.

It is run entirely as a Charity & costs her about 10. per. cent. on the sales – she has regular customers & seems to have no difficulty in selling – no web being sold under 4/- a yard. & mostly at 4/6. – hose & yarn she deals in very little, as they entail so much trouble.

As it is, it means working at it two days a week or four hours a day from the beginning of July till the end of October – and the rest of the year an average of one day a week – At Christmas time she gets an accountant to come for 4 or 5 days & works with him herself.

Till this year she has had half a stall for tweeds at the Highland & Agricultural Society's Show for the 3 or 4 days – the other half of the stall being taken by a Mrs Traill who sells Shetland goods –

This stall Lady Fowler means no longer to go on with, & says that either the Cooperative Council or *Comunm Gàidhealach* might like to take possession of it – It used to cost about £30 to run it – & was a very good advertisement for the tweeds – she had a salesman & an accountant there as they were found to be a necessity –

Weds. 4th Dec.

Left Inverbroom – motored all the way to Muir of Ord & arrived at Kilcoy in the Evening.

Travelling – Stationery & Postage Expenses from Sunday. 17th. Nov. to Sunday 8th. Dec 1912.

		£	s.	d.
	Carried forward	18.	11.	8.
Hiring.	Single horse waggonette Strath to Point		15.	
	do do do do to Hotel (day of leaving)		2.	6.
	Coach Gairloch to Achnasheen		9.	
Train	Achnasheen to Garve		1.	4.
	Muir. of. Ord to Redcastle			3 ½
	Porters			9.
Stationery.	Note book for Industry orders			6.
	Bottles black & red ink for stylo pens		1.	4.
	"Stones Envelopes" for holding letters etc (5).		2.	
	Subscription to "Oban Times" (sent 7/6 not knowing the right amount, have so far received no paper & no receipt for the money – written to inquire why)		7.	6.
Telegram.	Lady Fowler			6.
Post. cards.	Lexie MacLeod, Dalibrog, S.Uist (about stockings) (2)			1.
	Postmaster Killearnan			½
	Mrs MacLean, Isle of Grimsay			½
Letters.	"Oban Times" (2)			2.
	Hon. Sec. (7)			7.
	Factor Dunvegan			1.
	Lady Marjorie MacKenzie			1.
	Miss MacKenzie, Farr, (about order for yarn)			1.
	Ferguson, Lochboisdale			1.
	Lady Fowler (2)			2.
	MacLaren, Stationer, Inverness. (2)			2.
	Annie Macdonald, Teacher, Kilmuir			1.
	Mrs Stewart, Cupar Fife. (2)			2.
	Mrs Burnley Campbell. (2).			2.
	Rev. MacDonald, Kilmuir.			1.
	Maud Rose, Bayhead, N. Uist			1.
	Carried forward	20.	14.	6 ½
Letters (continued).	Editor, Irish Homestead Newspaper, (about price of tweeds)			1.
	Miss MacKintosh, Creagorry, Benbecula (knitting order) (2)			2.
	Miss Rickett, Seaford, Sussex (knitting & drugget order) (2)			2.

		£	s.	d.
	Miss Campbell, Kilberry,			1.
	John MacPherson, Northbay, Isle of Barra.			1½.
	Mrs Patten MacDougall.			1.
	Miss MacKenzie, Dunvegan, (Factor's sister)			1.
	MacIver, Achnasheen.			1.
	Manager Garve Hotel			1.
	Miss Champion, St Andrews (knitting order)			1.
	Mrs Hamilton Campbell			1.
	Rev. Lamont, Broadford			1.
	Rev. Morrison, Stornoway.			1.
	Mrs MacLean, Isle of Grimsay. (2)			2.
	Sending postal order for £1.12. 6. to above (tweed sold)			3.
	Fraser, Solicitor Portree (telling him about price of wool)			1.
	MacIver, Merchant, Strath.			1.
	Tina MacIntyre, do			1.
	Mrs MacAskill, Factor, Gairloch.			1.
	Mrs Boyd, Milton Farm, South Uist			
Sundries.	Mrs Boyd for knitting 2 pairs of pattern stockings from the yarn bought from Widow Fraser, Clachan		4.	0.
	Postage of parcel.			4.
	1lb of yarn spun by Mrs Norman MacQuien Carinish, North Uist at 2/9 (this yarn has been knitted into 2 pairs of socks for Miss Warrand's Canadian orders & the money will be refunded by her to the Council)		2.	9.
		21.	3.	9.
(forgotten)	Registered letter to Vancouver B.C. to Miss Myra Warrand containing "Bill of Lading" of the St Kilda. Tweeds.			4.
		21.	4.	1.
	Carried forward	21	4	1.
	Tip to Inverbroom Motor man			
Train	Redcastle to Edinburgh			
10th Dec.	Cab from station to Moray Place Edin.			
	Taxi to station for Glasgow			
	Cab to station leaving Edinburgh			
		22.	8.	2.

Acknowledgements

I wish to thank the institutions and public bodies for the research facilities they provide in my work as Director and Collector for the Vanishing Scotland Archive. After nearly forty years of collecting I am now concentrating on publishing from the archive to give a wider audience access to this unique material. The hope is that a permanent home may be found in the coming years for the archive, giving access to the ethnological material for future generations.

The Hebridean section of the archive contains the original source material pertaining to the work of the Highland and Scottish Home Industries. The collecting from current oral sources continues and would not be possible without the generosity of the contribution from each individual.

Institutions and organisations in particular are: The School of Scottish Studies, Historic Environment Scotland, National Library of Scotland, Register House National Records of Scotland, Highland Archives Inverness, University of Aberdeen Archives, Mitchell Library, Kildonan Museum, Stove Collective, Dumfries.

I would also like to thank the following individuals for their support and encouragement during this project and throughout the years,and to everyone who has appreciated and valued the work of the Vanishing Scotland Archive:

The informants from Berneray, North Uist, South Uist, Eriskay, Skye and the mainland of Scotland.

Alasdair Cameron, Dr Allan Turner, Murdo Turner, Jean Rodger, Malcolm Bangor Jones, Isobel and Sandy Reid, John Purser, Dr John MacInnes, Hamish Henderson, Gina MacDonald, Mairi Macleod, Dr Margaret Bennett, Dr Christopher Lee, Jackie Lee, Ailsa Watson, Ninian Crichton Stuart, Marietta Crichton Stuart, Elaine Kennedy, and Kara Millen for mentorship and research and my Family who continue to support my life and work.

Appendices

APPENDIX A
Highland Home Industries

APPENDIX B
Reproduction of a Scottish Home Industries Pamphlet

APPENDIX C
The mystery of Isabell: Who was she?

APPENDIX D
The Bigger Picture

APPENDIX E
The Diary

Appendix A.

Highland Home Industries

In 1909 Mr Eoghan Carmichael (son of Alexander Carmichael, author of *Carmina Gadelica*) and Miss Campbell of Inverneill, (Hon.Secretary) were deputed to get in touch with all the various Home Industries (HHI) and the result was the formation of The Co-operative Council of the Highland Home Industries. The Marchioness of Bute was president and Sir Kenneth MacKenzie of Gairloch, Hon. Treasurer.

The first aim of this body was to raise the standard of Home Industry work generally and Miss Isabell Burton MacKenzie was appointed as their Travelling Organiser from 1911 to 1914.

> 'She was a great friend of Lady Marjory MacKenzie, and though quite untrained in business methods, she was sympathetic and had vision. She did an immense amount of spadework in the Outer Isles and Skye. Her diaries were most interesting, and what was more important still , she made a very full register of the workers- spinners,knitters and weavers in the Outer Isles'[1]

1. Extract from a 'History of Growth of Highland Home Industries' document in the Vanishing Scotland Archive Collection)

North and South Uist, Berneray, Barra and Skye were now to be visited by Isabell the first Organiser of the Co-operative Council of Highland Home Industries. The account she gives us of the Autumn of 1912 is the only legacy left from her time as Organiser, apart from a letter she wrote to the Edinburgh Newspaper, *The Scotsman* asking the general public to help the plight of the nearly destitute women and children in the Western Isles, as their menfolk have gone to War.

It is a highly unusual and insightful diary.

In 1912 the Tweed Industry was collapsing and the landless tenants of the Crofts of the Highlands and Islands were experiencing great hardship. Making a living in the Outermost Isles of Berneray, North and South Uist, Eriskay and Barra was particularly difficult, being so remote and the people were enduring a subsistence economy on poor land. The brutal clearances of the indigenous people from the better land was within living memory and creation of the Scottish Home Industries (SHI) Board was an attempt by the land owning and professional classes along with the merchants to give a legitimate trade for homespun cloth and other craft industries.

The roots of this organisation lay in the 19th century, with their patron – H.R.H. Princess Louise daughter of Queen Victoria. By 1901 they had spread out from their London depot, establishing two in mainland Scotland with Lady Rosebery as president and three in the Outer Hebrides, under the presidency of the Duchess of Sutherland.

In 1914 at the outbreak of the First World War the SHI was dissolved and the depots in London and the Hebrides closed down. However, the HHI continued to thrive until well into the second half of the twentieth century.

The impact of World War 1 on the islands was devastating. It took away most of the menfolk and left many of the women and children destitute and starving in a subsistence culture where the products of their labour – tweeds, knitted goods and crafts made from the materials from the land, were integral to their survival.

In September 1914, Isabell felt that the situation was so dire that she wrote a letter to *The Scotsman* newspaper from Kilcoy headed 'APPEAL FROM HEBRIDEAN WOMEN'. She wrote:

> 'If orders for knitting socks and belts for soldiers at the front could be sent to those islands, it would be an immense boon to the women and girls; nearly all the men are away either in the Regular Army, Naval Reserve, Lovat Scouts, or Territorials, while the women are left to work the crofts and get through the winter as best they can.'(*The Scotsman* 1914).

There was little chance of them selling the shooting and golfing stockings because of the war and 'their own industry of tweed-making is almost at a standstill, as no sales taking place'* and thus Isabel suggests sending the orders to her, for her to arrange the knitting and dispatching of the orders.

She talks about the quality of the yarn that the women spin, and that socks made of this wool are 'splendid for rough wear' and are remarkably 'warmer than shop-wool ones'*.

'The yarn can be had in the natural shades of the wool – browns, greys, and white.'*
She gives detailed amounts and costs, as follows:
'Three cuts of yarn make two pairs of socks'
…and…
'Homespun yarn,………1s. per cut
Homespun socks,……....2s. per pair

Alloa socks, ………….1s. 9d. per pair
Homespun belts,……..2s. each
Alloa belts,…………...1s. 9d. each'

(*The Scotsman* 1914)

She adds that she has just returned from the islands and has witnessed 'numbers of men leaving and watched with admiration the quiet heroism of the women, who let them go without a murmur.' *

* Quotes above from Isabell's letter to *The Scotsman* Newspaper, 1914. *See also*: *The Scotsman* (1860-1920); Sept 26, 1914; ProQuest Historical Newspapers: *The Scotsman* (1817-1950) p. 8.

This facsimile of a pamphlet, compiled by the Duchess of Sutherland, gives some history of the SHI organisation and contemporary thought process which laid the foundation for the HHI.

The Story of a Highland Industry.*

By the DUCHESS OF SUTHERLAND.

"My day it wears onward 'twixt spinning and weaving,
The noise of men's laughter, the cry 'of their grieving
Drifts slow by my thorn-tree like drifting of snow,
And on the old branches the new blossoms blow."

REMARKABLE in its wonderful scientific discoveries, few can deny that the nineteenth century in this country has made for ugliness. The hideous factories, the machinery, the squalid dwellings; of great cities vividly support the assertion.

Only during the last decade a revulsion of feeling has arisen. The Sleeping Beauty has slept her sleep; the Fairy Prince, in the form of enlightened public opinion, has struggled over every obstacle nearer to her arms; and the last of the great prophets of the century, John Ruskin, will go down to his grave knowing that his labours and those of his co-workers - Carlyle, Morris, Rossetti, and the rest-have not been altogether in vain; that their splendid condemnations and appreciations will bear fruit in a dawning era. Men's eyes see again, men's minds live again, men's hands fashion again.

Already the revival of handicrafts which flourished in the fifteenth and sixteenth centuries is taking root throughout Great Britain. At the Home Arts and Industries Annual Exhibition in the Albert Hall in London are to be found exquisite book-binding from Uhiswick, specimens of the Della Robia pottery from Birkenhead, fine hand-woven linen from the Ruskin Industry at Keswick, and so many other presentments indicative of this growing artistic feeling that it would be impossible to enumerate them here.

In these efforts there is no headstrong ambition, for, to use the wise sentences of Mr. I.A. Hobson, the economist, "It is, in a word, a practical informal attempt of a civilised society to mark out for itself the reasonable limits of machine-production, and to insist that 'cheapness' shall not dominate the whole industrial world to the detriment of the pleasure and benefit arising from good work to the worker and consumer. Such a movement neither hopes nor seeks to restore mediævalism in industry, nor does it profess hostility to machinery, but it insists that machines shall be confined to the heavy, dull, monotonous, and therefore inhuman processes of work, while for the skill of human hand and eye shall be preserved all work which is pleasant and educative in its doing, and the skill and character of which contribute pleasure and profit to its use."

Yet, in connection with all this, by sheer force of circumstances, the home industries of Harris and Lewis, of Shetland, of Sutherland, and other parts of the Highlands, stand somewhat aloof in a sense; through their tremendous importance they pass from the mere question of art and sentiment to a serious problem.

The people of the Highlands and Islands have little land to cultivate. Their homes, most of them still built after a primitive fashion - thick stone walls, thatched roof, no chimney, tiny loopholes for windows - cling to the rocky sides of hills. Enter any of these cabins, and through the wreaths of blue curling peat smoke there will ever be seen an old woman seated spinning by the fire, and beyond, in the corner, the family loom, where the women of the house spend so many laborious hours in their struggle for daily bread, while the men "follow the sea", a precarious way of life.

The industry of these crofters and cottars is beautiful and useful. That is unquestionable. It has existed since time immemorial, from Ossianic days, when one

> '. . . . . came slowly from the setting sun
> To Erer of Borda, in her clay piled Dun,
> And found her dyeing cloth with subtle care."

But, more than this, the success or failure of the industry at the present time means life or death to a people; that over-mastering power-machinery - has taken it by the throat and written extinction in grim letters on its brow.

The Scottish Home Industries Association has been formed to combat this verdict; to ensure, with all the force of practical knowledge and sympathy, a legitimate trade for these people; to fight their battles against the ills of competition and "truck" - in fact, to keep open, for this generation at least, a wide channel for the distribution of the fascinating homespun cloth.

In a short article like this it is impossible to sum up every detail of its manufacture, or to find scope for a description of the legends connected with the pathetic surroundings of the workers. I would, however, transcribe as shortly as possible, for those who have not learnt Highland folk-lore and Highland customs at their grandma's knee, the processes of hand-spinning and hand-weaving.

The wool packets being opened out and roughly sorted or stapled according to quality and length of fibre, of which there is considerable variety in the same fleece, the wool is cleansed from the grease derived from contact with the sheep (and the various protective "dipping" or "bathing" processes to which that animal is in autumn subjected) by steeping in a hot liquid.

Dried and shaken up and still further "sorted", the wool is then passed through the process of carding or combing, to lay its fibres in the same direction. This is effected by means of a pair of implements like bair brushes, with the handles at the sides, and set with metal teeth.

It is now nearly ready to be spun into thread. The distaff and spindles were, from very early times, used for this purpose. The former is a staff, about four feet long, fixed in the waist-belt on the left side, or more commonly in the upturned outer skirt, which thus forms a pocket in front for carrying the clews or balls of thread. To the projecting head of the distaff the wool, previously cross-carded into inch-thick loose cylinders- in which the fibre has now assumed a sort of spiral arrangement - is tied in an open bunch or bundle. From this it is fed out of the left hand of the spinster to the spindle, which is held at starting in the right hand and afterwards swings from it. The spindle is a rounded piece of wood, about a foot long and half an inch in diameter, loaded at the lower end by the whorle, which acts as "fly-wheel", and is generally made of stone, often a disc of steatite, about the diameter of a bronze penny, and weighing over an ounce and a half.

Some wool, drawn out from the store on the distaff, to which it still remains attached, is twisted into a kind of thread and tied to the middle of the spindle, from which it passes upwards and is fastened - by a simple hitch to a notch near the spindle-head. This is then twirled by the right hand, and as it spins it twists up - as it is allowed to drop slowly towards the ground - all the wool to the distaff, the hands regulating the speed and further supply, and thus determining the thickness of the thread. From time to time the thread is coiled around the shaft of the spindle into a ball, and a new hitch made, till the clew is large enough to be slipped off, and a new one begun.

From the number of whorles found in connection with pre-historic remains in Scotland, their use must be very ancient, yet the spindle is still to be seen at work on the hillsides, employed for its original purpose of spinning. It is also used occasionally for twining together different colours of thread, when the spinning is done by the well known spinning-wheel. There are niceties about the use of this little machine, such as the adjustment of tensions, &c., which make some of the older workers as unwilling to let their unskilled daughters practise on it as a musical virtuoso would be to entrust his Cremona to a "scraper."

The next process is dyeing, and whether this is done "in the wool" or "in the thread," there is a final treatment in an ammoniacal liquid, called by the Highlanders "fual", which removes the last traces of oleaginous matter, and prepares the wool for receiving and retaining the dyes. The securing of uniformity of tint or shade has hitherto presented some difficulty, and this is partly due to the imperfection of the apparatus in common use, and to the usual habit of measuring the dyeing material merely by the handful. The ordinary dye-pot holds but a few hanks, and when the next batch of wool or thread is passed through a new decoction, and the tint tested by merely raising the streaming mass for a moment on the end of a stick, the effect in the web is often disappointing.

Technical instruction, however, has done much and will do more to improve this. Mineral dyes are now being used in conjunction with those of vegetable origin. A list of the latter, most of which are still in use, is here given as collected from various sources of information.

COLOUR	DYES.	BOTANICAL NAME.	GAELIC or NATIVE NAME.
Black	Alder-tree Bark	Alnus glutinosa	Rùsg Fearna
	Dock-root	Rumex obtusifolius ...	Bun-na-copaig
Blue	Bilberry (with alum) ...	Vacinnium myrtillus ...	Dearcan-Fraoich
	Elder (with alum)	Sambucus niger	Droman
Brown	Stone Lichen	Parmelia saxatilis ...	Crotal
	Dulse	Halymenia edulis	Duileasg,
	Currant (with alum) ...	Ribes ...	Preas-dearc
(yellowish) ...	Wall Lichen ...	Parmelia parietina ...	Crotal buidh
Crimson (bright)	Corcar Lichen ...	Lecanora Tartarea ...	Crotal-corcuia
	White Lichen ...	Lecanora palescens ...	Crotal-geal
(dark) ...	Dark Lichen ...	Parmelia ceratophylla ...	Crotal-dubh
Flesh-colour ...	Willow-bark	Salix viminalis ...	Cairt-sheilich
Grey	Iris-root	Iris pseud-acorus ...	Bun-an-t-Seilisdeir
Green	Broom	Genista tincturia	Bealaidh
	Furze-bark	Ulex Europacus	Rùisg-conuisg
	Heather (with alum) ...	Erica cinerea	Fraoch
Magenta	Dandelion	Leontodon taraxacum ...	Bearnan-Bride
Orange ... (dark) ...	Bramble	Rubus fructicosus	Preas-smour
Purple	Sundew	Drosera	Lus-na-fearnaich
Red ... (dark) ...	Rock Lichen	Ramalina scopulorum ...	Crotal-nan-Creag
(bright) ...	Rue-root	Galium verum	Bun-an-ruidh
Scarlet	Limestone Lichen ...	Urceolaria calcarea ...	Crotal clach-aoil
	Tormentil	Tormentilla officinalis ...	Leanartach
Violet	Watercress	Nasturtium officinalis ...	Biolaire
	Bitter Vetch	Orobus Tuberosus	Carmeal-ninnsinn
Yellow	Ash-tree Root	Fraxinus excelsior	Freumh-na-Craoichs
	Bracken-root	Pteris aqullina	Bun-na-Rainaich
(bright)	St. John's Wort	Hypericum Perforatum ...	Lus Chaluim-Chille
	Sun-dew (with ammonia)	Drosera	Lus-na-tearnaich
	Bog-myrtle	Myrica gale	Roid ...

The dyed thread, washed in salt water if blue, or in fresh if any other colour, is next woven into a web at the cottage hand-loom. Then comes the process of "felting" or thickening, called "wauking" in the North, probably from its being chiefly effected by the feet. The microscopic projections on the fibre interlock when the web is beaten wet, and as the "wauk-mill" is apt to overdo the work, turning out a texture hard, stiff and heavy, the old process is still preserved in the Highlands of Scotland, and secures a fabric soft, supple, and sufficiently dense to be wind-and-weather proof.

The following description is taken from a paper read before the Gaelic Society in 1885 :–

"In the Highland districts women make use of their feet to produce the same result [felting], and a picturesque sight it is to see a dozen or more Highland lassies sit ronnd in two rows facing each other. The web of cloth is passed round in a damp state, each one pressing it and pitching it with a dash to her next neighbour; and so the cloth is handled, pushed, crushed, and welded, so as to become close and even in texture. The process is slow and tedious, but the women know how to beguile the time, and the song is passed round, each one taking up the verse in turn, and all joining in the chorus. The effect is very peculiar, and often very pleasing, and the wauking songs are very popular in all the collections."

While to this method of "felting" the web something of the softness of the genuine homespun is due, it is also worthy of mention that the longer-stapled wools are less liable to become matted and hard under the thickening process, of whatever kind, than those which are of shorter fibre. Now it is onlywith the longer-fibred wool that the Highland wheel can work. Its very imperfection, then, as an instrument, or rather machine, becomes of advantage as a guarantee of durability, as well as of comfort in connection with the work which it turns out; for whereas the mill can use up almost any sort of wool, however short in the fibre and inferior in quality, the wheel can only use the best, and this is in the end the cheapest.

In conclusion, I come to the commercial and practical side of the whole question. We have an uphill struggle to find fresh markets for the cloth. Many a poor spinner has been turned away with clouded brow to carry the result of long weeks' toll to her cabin because the supply is exceeding the demand. Some English tradesmen tell us that most people nowadays prefer cheap and inferior doth, and that they will not pay heavy prices. This may be so, but I doubt it. A fair price for fair work all the world over!

Letters containing suggestions or questions, addressed to me as President of the Association, at our London Depot, 12, Woodstock Street, Oxford Street, London, W., will be gratefully considered and acknowledged. - *New Liberal Review*', August, 1901.

Edinburgh Depot: For Sale of Tweeds, Shetland Goods, &c.
Sutherland Depot: Golspie.
Outer Hebrides Depots: Tarbert. Harris and Stornoway.

Appendix C.

The Mystery of Isabell; Who was she?

Born. Aberdeen 1872 died Glasgow 1958.

Isabell was a pioneering single lady, and although born in Aberdeen her birth records were hard to find as her father Colonel John Burton Mackenzie was in the Military and she spent part of her early life in the South of England.

From birth to age forty when the diary begins, all we can glean thus far about her comes from her unique record of her life as the Travelling organiser for HHI.

She had three brothers and after the death of her father in 1901, continued to live at Kilcoy with her mother Isabella Jane. Her mother had inherited Kilcoy from her grandfather.

Isabell has exceptional skills as an artist and photographer as her deft pen and ink drawings scattered throughout the diary illustrate.

'She Kodaks people' *

Isabell had acquired the first small portable Kodak camera produced in 1912. This was to become known as "the soldiers camera", as it was used by soldiers and sailors who served in what was known as the Great War two years later.

* From 1912 to 1926, Kodak produced a small, portable camera called the Vest Pocket Photographic. It was nicknamed "the soldier's camera," in that millions of these little treasures were used by soldiers and sailors who served in what was then known as The Great War. 1914 to 1918.

She left the service of the Highland Home Industries just after the outbreak of War and worked during those years as a welfare supervisor for the Ministry of Munitions National Projectile factory near Glasgow. At St. James Palace on 1st January 1918 (reported in a supplement to the London Gazette) the King awarded her an MBE - a Member of the Most Excellent Order of the British Empire.

Appendix D.

The Bigger Picture

Widow MacPherson & Morag

Widow Fraser, Clachan

Spinners and Weavers, Isle of Berneray, Harris

Neil MacKintosh & MacSween

Mrs MacDonald, North Uist

A Crew of Barra Girls, Fish Curing Station

Young Outer Islanders

Appendix E.

The Diary

I was introduced to Isabell Burton MacKenzie through the pages of her diary by Miss Shand the last organiser of HHI. Miss Shand travelled the Islands for 27 years by bicycle from 1949 till 1976. Affectionately known as '*Cailleach Uighe*'- The Old Wool Woman - Miss Shand was accepted by the island people because of her skills, her cheery smile and sympathetic advice.

Isabell similarly speaks Gaelic fluently, often hiring a pony to visit crofters, and because of her meticulous book keeping , we get a sense of who people really are through her keen observances.

Within the pages of Isabell's diary and account book, she captures rare snapshots of everyday life in the Western Isles of Scotland, from the communal traditions of 'waulking the tweed' with it's haunting Gaelic songs to Willow Works and marble carving, woven grass horse collars and webs of cloth. The rhythm of the life of the Crofters dictated by weather and religious observances.

She also writes about the overwhelming power of the elements only found in these remote islands.

Today there are causeways which connect the islands to each other and ferries and boats with engine power. At the time of Isabell's journey there was constant vigilance around water crossings, the tides changed the landscape everyday and crossing Fords between the Islands was a tricky and dangerous business.

We have details of weather only found in these remote islands, and the overwhelming power the force of the elements have on the everyday lives of the Islanders. This is a landscape and seascape unlike any other place, at the edge of the Atlantic Ocean.

The last piece of the Isabell Burton MacKenzie mystery I found in the family graveyard at Kilcoy Castle. A gravestone with her dates and her fathers erected sometime after her death in 1958.

It has not been possible to cite all my research references here, but I would ask any reader who has information on HHI to contact me as I continue to delve into the remarkable lives of Isabell Burton Mackenzie and Miss Winifred Alured Shand.

Alyne Erskine Jones, is the Director of Vanishing Scotland, a network organization which promotes the understanding of Scottish Cultural Traditions. It is also home to a rich and unique ethnological archive, The Galloway Tryst, collected over the past four decades. The archive includes written, audio and visual records that give an insight into Cultural traditions through song, story, dance, language and indigenous knowledge.

Alyne lives and works as a cultural historian in South West Scotland. She has a teaching diploma in textiles from Queen's College, Glasgow and an MA Hons in Scottish Ethnology from Edinburgh University. She has taught, researched and collected for many years and received many research awards for her work, and this publication is the first to highlight her work in recording remarkable women.

The Vanishing Scotland Archive

www.vanishingyarns.co.uk

www.vanishingscotland.co.uk

Isabell Alicia Eva Burton MacKenzie, MBE
1872-1958

Index

Compiled by Peter Hamilton Currie – Member of the Society of Indexers

Page numbers in bold type denote the more important references; page numbers in italics denote illustrations or their captions; *passim* (e.g. 29-35 *passim*) conveys that the subject is referred to not continuously but in scattered passages throughout the pages; **q** stands for 'quoted' and **n** for 'notes'. In connection with dates: **b** – born; **d** – died; ***fl*** (*floruit*) – flourished; ***c*** (*circa*) – about (this date). Where other than Gaelic names are represented, they are done so in the manner commonly represented where English is spoken, with cross referencing to the native equivalents or variants thereof. The individual Western Isles are denoted thus: **Ba**-Barra; **Be**-Benbecula; **Bh**-Berneray, BHarris; **E**-Eriskay; **G**-Grimsay; **H**-Harris; **L**-Lewis; **M**-Mingulay; **S**-Skye; **Un**-Uist, North; **Us**-Uist, South; **V**-Vatersay; **W**-Wester Ross

F

G

H

I

J

K

L

M

N

O

T

U

V

W

X

Y

Z

Publications available from Vanishing Scotland

by **Alyne E. Jones**

Travelling People and the Tinkler Gypsies of Galloway

A compelling collection of photographs and overview of the ethos of the travelling people, their society, beliefs and way of life. Inspired by a unique collection of Galloway photographs, the author has delved deep into the Ethnology of the travelling people — the oral tradition is central to their culture and the author was privileged to count many fine singers and storytellers amongst her friends.

Traditional Scottish Knitting

Sanquhar Pattern Gloves

The Sanquhar Pattern is a unique style of knitting, both distinctive and durable. Created by local knitters in a small town in Southern Scotland. It first appears in historical records nearly 200 years ago. The secrets of the Sanquhar pattern have been passed on by word of mouth from generation to generation. This booklet gives us fascinating glimpses into the life of an ancient Scottish Burgh over the centuries and provides full instructions on how to knit a pair of Traditional Scottish Gloves, in the Sanquhar pattern.

Forthcoming Publications from Vanishing Scotland

by Alyne E. Jones

Knitting by Bicycle

The Story of the last organiser for the Highland Home Industries in the Hebrides.

Between 1949 and 1976, Miss Shand, was the last organiser for the Highland Home Industries in Scotland, travelling 20,000 miles around the Outer Hebrides on her ancient Raleigh bike.

Affectionately known by the Gaelic speaking Islanders as *Cailleach Uighe* - The Old Wool Woman. she was an expert spinner and dyer and had written about Hebridean dyes for International publications.

Her collection of photographs give us a glimpse of a vanished world, where intrepid journeys were required, often wading across shallow water with her shoes tied around her neck!

Part of Miss Shand's legacy was an extensive array of contemporary newspaper cuttings and letters which give the flavour of the Hebrides during the 50's and 60's including the controversial rocket range, the Queen's visit just after her coronation, and cameos of islanders at work contrasted with prestigious national shows.

Travelling between the worlds of high fashion and remote Scottish crofts, it was her job to tell the weavers spinners and knitters what was needed in the fashion capitals of commerce.